Cyrus Elder

Dream of a Free-Trade Paradise

And Other Sketches

Cyrus Elder

Dream of a Free-Trade Paradise
And Other Sketches

ISBN/EAN: 9783744724197

Printed in Europe, USA, Canada, Australia, Japan.

Cover: Foto ©Thomas Meinert / pixelio.de

More available books at **www.hansebooks.com**

OF A

FREE-TRADE PARADISE,

AND

OTHER SKETCHES.

BY

CYRUS ELDER.

WITH 12 ILLUSTRATIONS OF HENRY L. STEPHENS.

—————••••————

PHILADELPHIA:
PUBLISHED FOR THE INDUSTRIAL LEAGUE.
BY
HENRY CAREY BAIRD,
INDUSTRIAL PUBLISHER,
406 WALNUT STREET.
1872.

5

WHAT THE COUNTRY WANTS.

"A DUTY only upon those articles which we could dispense with, known as luxuries, and those of which we use more than we produce."

"All duty removed from tea, coffee, and other articles of universal use not produced by ourselves."

"Encouragement to home products, employment to labor at living wages, and development of home resources."

"Disappearance of the national tax-gatherer, and reduction of the national debt."

President Grant's Message.

6

PREFACE.

THESE sketches, which discuss and illustrate, in a humorous or familiar style, a subject popularly regárded as heavy, and which is "*caviare* to the general," have been printed anonymously, from time to time, during the last four years, and are now republished in book form, in the hope that they will lead the reader to the study of better and graver writings on the great theme of National Welfare.

THE AUTHOR.

JOHNSTOWN, PENNA.,
June 5, 1872.

7

CONTENTS.

LIST OF ILLUSTRATIONS.

10

DREAM OF A FREE-TRADE PARADISE.

A Laissez Faire Tale.

NOTE.—"*Laissez faire*" is a French phrase nearly equivalent to "let alone"—much used by Free-Traders to express their doctrine, that things should be allowed to take their own course without protection or restraint by law.

I AM a hard-worked professor in a Western college, and, among other things, I teach political economy. Wayland's is our text-book; and having committed it to memory years ago, and made a good many boys memorize and recite it, I am a Free-Trader, of course. I used to have no trouble, but of late there is a good deal of bother with it. The boys read the newspapers out of school, and General Schenck's speeches, and Senator Scott's speeches, and other publications, give them ideas not in the book, and they ask questions sometimes that are hard to answer.

I thought it would be well to study up a little during vacation, so I got several speeches on the free-trade side, and I read one of them in the cars the other day. After I finished it, I undertook to read the platform of principles of the Free-Trade League, but I found in it much food for thought, and made but slow progress. Every proposition tended to one thing—cheapness; and though I believe, of course, that to "buy where you can buy cheapest" is the first maxim of political economy, I was not just then so much concerned about where or how I would buy, as about the sale of my labor for the coming year. I had expected to be re-engaged at the college, of course, but a down-east professor had offered his services at a good deal less per year than I was receiving. Self-respect would not allow me to bid against him, and I believed the trustees would prefer home industry to foreign industry that was untried; but I could not help thinking, suppose they should conclude to "buy where they could buy cheapest?" What, in that case, would become of me?

One proposition, however, pleased me greatly. It was this:
"Every country has its peculiar natural advantages, and to

Where all must shovel and hoe, wages must be low.

11

Diversified industry is a defence against famine.

THE PROFESSOR IN THE CAR.

produce what can be most easily produced in it, and to exchange such products for what is more easily produced elsewhere, is the most profitable exertion of industry."

Here, I thought, is an idea that admits of indefinite extension. " Every country "—that means the people, of course; and as the rule should apply to every man, for the nation is composed of individuals, it follows that instead of trying to coerce nature, every person should respect the bent of his genius by pursuing his natural advantages, that is, do whatever comes easiest for him. There are my school boys, for instance; why should they be hammering away at the hardest tasks; and men—why should they consider it meritorious to overcome great obstacles? Why shouldn't they all do the easiest things?

Just here we went through a tunnel, and I asked an intelligent stranger beside me how long it was.

" Nearly a mile," said he.

" Couldn't they get around this place?" I asked.

" Yes," said he, " but it took four miles to do it."

The rewards of labor increase as occupations become diversified.

" Well, but it seems to me, that it would have been easier and cheaper to go around than to make such an enormous work as this?"

" You are right, sir; it would have been easier and cheaper to do it the first time, or for a year, or perhaps ten years; but when you consider the saving of that three miles of distance to all the trains that travel over this road in twenty, thirty, or forty years, the tunnel is the best investment the company have made, for it overcomes the difficulty once for all. It's like the tariff that makes us pay something for a few years to build up manufactories, which then give us a more plentiful supply of cheaper goods than we could ever get in any other way."

Ah, thought I, here is one of those Pennsylvania monopolists that I have so often heard about. Of course I did not answer him, but looked out of the car window, where I saw a man grubbing away on a very rough piece of land; and while I was wondering if he intended to sow wheat, and how stupid it was of him, and why he didn't buy his wheat, or go somewhere else where it was easier to raise it, I fell fast asleep.

On awaking I found myself lying on the grass in a little grove, and near me was sitting a venerable man, clad in a closely-fitting suit of fur, and engaged in reading a newspaper, from which he glanced occasionally to regard me with kindly interest.

Surprised, but in no way alarmed, I gathered myself up, and my companion also arising with a friendly nod, I took it upon myself to open a conversation.

" Will you be kind enough to tell me where I am?" said I.

" Sir," said the venerable being, "you are now in the happy country of *Laissez Faire*, where the laws interfere in no way with the employments of the people, and everybody does what is easiest to him. The present government was established by free-trade philosophers, and is now in the hands of Special Commissioners, of whom I am highest in authority."

" Judging from your literary appearance," said I, "you must also be at the head of some institution of learning; and being a teacher myself, I would be glad to know on what principle your schools are conducted."

" On the principle of doing what is easiest," said he. "A boy, for instance, finds it difficult to learn arithmetic, but quite easy to go fishing. He therefore goes fishing. Of course he is a poor scholar, but he probably becomes a good fisherman."

" How are the schools supported?" I asked; "is there a school tax?"

The introduction of manufactures diversifies agriculture.

THE PROFESSOR AWAKING.

"Oh, no," he replied, "that is one of the heresies of the doctrine of Protection, long since discarded here. It wont do to tax one class for the benefit of another; and besides, government has nothing to do with education. The let-alone policy is the best. Every man pays for his own schooling, and the schools are not crowded, for we recognize the folly of wasting time and trouble with the mass of children who can never become as clever as the few who have natural genius for some branch of study. We attend to the latter, and let the others pursue some employment for which they possess natural advantages."

"Might not the dull pupils, however," I asked, "if labored with and encouraged, eventually develop powers which would enable them to excel; or, if not, is not the discipline of study of value to all?"

"That is another heresy of the doctrine of Protection," he replied. "There is more profit in doing what comes easiest, and such experiments are costly. In this country, cheapness is the

The Earth is a machine given to man to be fashioned for his purposes.

principal consideration, and cheapness and easiness are convertible terms."

" I presume you have no regular course of study, then, for all pupils?" said I.

" No, sir," said he; "and we have discarded several branches which were in vogue in early days. Geography, for instance, is not taught. How absurd it was for a child to spend several years of labor, and a teacher as much of toil, at great expense to the parent, for the purpose of memorizing the facts of this science, when a few pence will purchase a book containing them fully. The child would never be able to remember all the facts in the book, at any rate. To go to memory for such things is a costly and laborious way: to go to the book is easy and cheap, and we prefer it, of course."

Passing from the grove, we entered upon an exceedingly rough, and, indeed, almost impassable road, which conducted us into a small valley, watered by a considerable stream. Observing on the way that the land seemed to have been at one time cultivated, but was now abandoned and grown up with weeds and a young forest, I asked my conductor what it meant.

" Before our Board of Commissioners came in power," said he, " the policy of doing the easiest thing was not understood, and some foolish people had made farms around here; but the soil is naturally poor, and the commissioners obliged them to quit and go over to the other side of the country, which possesses natural advantages for agricultural pursuits."

" Might not this soil, by cultivation, have been made fertile?" I asked.

" Some stupid people maintained this," he replied, "and it was asserted that if the farmers would dig down a number of feet to the limestone, quarry it out, burn it, and spread it on the land, great crops might be produced; but such absurdity could not be encouraged. It would cost too much; and, besides, the business of a farmer is to farm, not to quarry stone or turn lime-burner."

" How did they take the matter?" said I; "did they object to removing?"

" Some did," said he; "but after the stupid business in the valley below us was stopped, all were glad to go. Most of them went over to the other side on the rich lands, but they are a grumbling set, and complain that the rich lands are worked out, and are poorer than these hill-sides."

Passing along, we presently came to a bend in the stream,

where the valley opened out, and here I saw some ancient ruins which looked like the remains of a furnace, dwelling-houses, and other buildings.

"What is this place?" said I.

"Another triumph of our commissioners," said my companion. "In the former reign of which I spoke, it had been usual to send a fleet of boats twice a year to a large island across the sea, to obtain iron and a variety of implements of the chase and of war, for which were traded the gold and silver in which this country is so very rich. But some curious fellows discovered in these hills veins of rough stone, out of which they declared iron could be made; and they engaged to furnish all that would be needed, and a great deal more than was usually consumed, if the Government would ensure them a sale for it at a fair price. The authorities knew no better than to give such a guarantee, and the work went on. Hundreds of workmen were employed in digging ore and smelting it, and the manufacture of various implements out of the native iron was begun, and the work was progressing on a large scale when the Special Commissioners came into power. Of course they soon found out that iron-making was one of the hardest things to do; and, besides, the iron cost too much, and the Government guarantee was annulled."

"Well, could not the works go on without that?" I asked.

"Oh, no," said he; "it was tried for a while, but the boats brought in a lot of cheaper iron, and the business was abandoned, as was right, and the workers resorted to more productive industries."

"What were they, for instance, if I may ask?"

"Farming the rich land on the other side of the country," he replied. "Of course the grumbling farmers over there complained about so many more coming into the business, and said that it made food so cheap nobody wanted to buy it, which was absurd, of course. The first duty of Government is to see that everything is made cheap, and cheap food is the most important of all. There were other factories, but when the iron went down, they went down also, as was right, of course. The country has no natural advantages for manufacturing, and it is easier and cheaper to get goods from over the sea, where they know how to make everything."

"I should think," said I, "that such remarkable changes could not be made without some trouble, and a great deal of suffering."

"It was all in accordance with nature," said he. "We hold

Labor is the original purchase-money for all things having exchangeable value.

THE GREAT PEANUT SPEECH.

that any industry that cannot sustain itself ought to perish. One man ought not to be taxed to sustain the business of another. There was a pestilent party that argued strongly to us, that we should encourage the making of iron, but the peanut argument shut them up."

"The peanut argument," said I; "what is that?"

"Did you never read my great speech entitled, 'A plea for the peanut, or principles of protective political economy?'" he inquired.

"Never," said I.

"You have lost something, then," said he. "I showed how many acres of land in the country would grow peanuts, and how many tons could be produced to the acre, if the Government would only give a bounty for every bushel raised, and what amount of tax it would be on every man, woman, and child in the country; and when the iron-makers came forward with their claims, I put in my plea for the protection of peanuts, and, of course, the absurdity of the whole business was seen by everybody."

"Did no one suggest," I asked, "that in a national point of view, the production of pig-iron and of peanuts might not be equally important?"

"Well, yes, that suggestion was made, but we laughed it down," said he.

As we passed further along into the valley, I was surprised to find no signs of habitation, and observed to my companion that as yet I had seen no dwelling-houses.

"Certainly not," said he. "We long ago gave over building them, for we found out that it was much easier to live in caves in the ground, than to employ a variety of workmen in getting together materials and erecting houses. It is more in accordance with the natural advantages of the country. Besides being costly, buildings are not really necessary, for people are not as plentiful as they used to be."

"Oh, indeed; and what is the reason of that?" I asked.

"There are a number of causes for it," he replied. "There were at one time too many of them, but a large number left the country, which was a good thing, of course. Then, as the farmers had discovered that it was easier to grow peanuts than any other crop, they quit raising everything else, which was all right. It happened, however, that there came a bad peanut year, and a good many people died, which was fortunate, as it was not nearly so easy for the commissioners to find food for them as to bury them."

I had been so much interested in my companion's discourse, that I had not noted the lapse of time, and now suggested to him that I might be detaining him from his duties.

"O, no," said he, "I am not much employed just now, for there is no school."

"Indeed," said I, "and why not?"

"It is, in point of fact," said he, "because there are no children."

"No children," I exclaimed, "and why not?"

"The commissioners discovered that men were about the most costly product of the country," he replied. "During long years of infancy they had to be fed and cared for, yet could do nothing; and to clothe and teach them was also a tremendous labor and expense; while, on the other hand, a cow, ox, or horse was serviceable or fit for food in a few years. So the commissioners determined that it was easier to produce other animals, and

"NO CHILDREN."

cheaper to get men already full grown from over the seas.   The birth of children had already fallen off greatly, for the commissioners had been long opposed to encouraging a surplus of population, and by judiciously strangling or drowning such children as appeared, the product soon ceased.   The scheme worked admirably, with the exception that the stupid people over the seas cannot now be induced to come here."

"Then," said I, in amazement, "you have no grown people, either?"

"No," said he, "none whatever.   The commissioners survived everybody else, and I survived them, and you see in me all the theoretical beauties of free-trade philosophy reduced to practice, and perfectly illustrated."

More amazed than ever, I scrutinized my companion more closely, and now observed that what I had taken for a neat dress of animal fur, was really his own skin, covered with a growth of hair, and discolored in places by exposure to the weather.   I noticed, too, for the first time, that the papers which had helped to impress me with his literary character were a copy of the New York *Evening Post*, and the last Report of Hon. D. A. Wells, United States Special Commissioner of Revenue.

" Dear professor," said I, " I observe that the country of *Laissez Faire* still maintains some trade with the outer world; yet, as you at this time seem to produce nothing, I am at a loss to know what you give in exchange for your favorite literature."

" It is sent to me gratis by the Free-Trade League," he replied.

At this moment I heard a distant noise, which grew in intensity until I recognized a sound which belongs not to the country of *Laissez Faire*—it was a steam whistle. While puzzling over this incongruity, with a sudden jerk the cars stopped, and I awoke from my dream.

PIG-IRON AND POTATOES.

THE Revenue Reformers desire to put on the free list every article which can be produced by home labor, and to raise all the revenue from customs, by duties on tea, coffee, and such other things as are wholly of foreign origin. Their scheme is set forth at great length in an essay, which Mr. Asper, a Representative from Missouri in the last Congress, contributed to the columns of the *Congressional Globe*, and it is sufficiently plausible to justify the outcry against "manufacturing monopolists," raised by the ignorant followers of the Free-Trade League.

The proposition of Mr. Asper is that when a duty is imposed upon an article we cannot or do not produce, its effect ends with its payment, but should it be our misfortune to be able to produce the article in this country, then the cost of the domestic product is enhanced to the full amount of the duty, and the poor consumers pay this tax to the bloated manufacturing monopolists. For instance, he says, "we imported during the last fiscal year $19,-000,000 worth of cottons at an average duty of 42½ per cent., which brought to the Treasury $8,100,000. That during the same time there were manufactured in the United States of cotton goods $242,100,000 worth, the price of which, to the consumer, was enhanced $92,450,000, which, paying 3½ per cent. of tax into the Treasury, leaves 30 per cent. of increased prices, which fell on the consumer!" It is plain to Mr. Asper that the bloated cotton manufacturers have been pocketing about three cents on every yard of ten-cent calico or muslin they have sold during the past year, over and above the price they should have received, and that if the duty were repealed we should at once buy ten-cent calico and muslin at about seven cents!* That is Mr. Asper's idea

---

* "In the debates of '44—'46 it was shown that in 1816 there was a duty of about seven cents a square yard imposed on cotton goods then selling at twenty-five and thirty cents per yard, by a bill reported by Mr. Lowndes and advocated by Mr. Calhoun, of S. C., and that afterwards a duty of $4 per box was put on glass, three and a half cents per pound on nails, etc., which at the time of the debate appeared to be selling, cotton for six cents a yard, glass at $3½ a box, nails at three and a quarter cents a pound, etc. Yet it was still contended, then as now, that the duty was added to the price and paid by the consumer. That is, that the consumer who bought a yard of domestic cotton for six cents paid seven cents duty; on a box of glass he bought for $3.50 he

---

Civil liberty is the child of prosperous industry.

of the thing, and he elaborates it statistically in a wonderful way, showing how much cottons, woollens, iron, salt, boots, paper, etc., are imported; how much domestic product consumed, what tax is paid to the Government in duties, and what tax is paid to the monopolists in prices, bringing out a result which would have amazed anybody but Mr. Asper, but which he states with a beautiful statistical simplicity. It is $336,200,000 that the people pay the monopolists because of the tariff—a trifling sum, which Mr. Asper would save by repeal of the duty!

We are more than ever anxious to know the mathematical Mark Twain who fabricates such astounding statistics for unsophisticated members of Congress. What a joy he must feel in seeing his jokes printed at large in the *Congressional Globe*, at the expense of the Government.

We have to complain that Mr. Asper did not carry his calculations a little further. True, we are more than ruined, but if he had footed up the millions of dollars which the duty of ten cents a bushel on Indian corn obliges the consumers to pay to the bloated farmers to enable the Treasury to collect in the fiscal year of 1869 the pitiful sum of $5,045.09; and the other millions of dollars which the duty of twenty-five cents a bushel on imported potatoes draws from the pockets of the hard working mechanics of the country, by increasing in that amount the price of all the potatoes consumed by them, with other atrocities of like nature, he would have caused our two eyes, like stars, to start from their spheres, and we would have probably discerned that the tariff had not only ruined the country, but also impoverished the human race. We have no bureau, and have not yet been able to hire a statistician, but we cannot resist the temptation to extend Mr. Asper's table for him. We have changed but one word in his heading—manufacturers, we have made to read farmers, and we beg of you, oh, our countrymen, to look upon it and weep.

Here are but seven agricultural products on which the people are taxed for the benefit of the grasping, greedy farmers, the enormous sum of nearly one hundred and eighty millions of dollars per annum, for the purpose of putting little more than a million of dollars into the Treasury :—

paid $4 duty; on a pound of nails he bought for three and a quarter cents, he paid a duty of three and a half cents. These facts were not denied, but the theory had to be maintained, that the duty was added to the price or all their speeches about taxation oppression, etc., would have vanished into air."—*Hon. Andrew Stewart of Penna. Letter to Hon. Jas. G. Blaine, April 10th, 1872.*

The nearer the producer to the consumer the larger the product.

TABLE A.—*Showing the amount of Imports and domestic Products consumed in the United States in the fiscal year 1869, with Duties and amounts paid into the Treasury, with the amount of Bounties paid to the farmer.*

ARTICLES.	Total consumption with duties addded.	Imported from foreign countries.	Home products consumed.	Av'g rate Duty	Revenue paid to Government.	Enhanced amount paid to monopolists.
Wheat.,	$222,008,181 20	$1,270,588 35	$220,540,861	15½	$196,731 35	$34,183,833 45
Rye	21,934,562 55	97,080 10	21,821,337	16⅔	16,145 45	3,655,073 94
Oats	137,187,143 63	119,630 27	137,041,222	21⅔	26,291 36	29,806,465 78
Indian Corn	651,783,064 85	72,254 00	651,711,981	12¼	8,328 85	70,835,817 67
Barley	29,989,129 29	5,873,139 61	23,341,719	11½	774,270 68	2,684,297 08
Buckwheat	15,816,925 50	2,418 64	15,814,265	10	241 86	158,142 65
Potatoes	71,313,473 71	80,396 46	71,200,295	40⅔	32,785 25	29,014,120 20
Totals					$1,055,295 80	$179,336,851 37

A tax for the benefit of the farmer of $4.65 on each inhabitant; $27.90 on a family of six persons.

We might have extended this table by including butter, which pays a duty of four cents a pound; cheese, which pays the same; hops, which pays five cents per pound; honey taxed thirty-six and a half per cent., and peanuts—the favorite dessert of Hon. S. S. Cox, whose plea for the peanut ranks with the finest specimens of classic oratory—peanuts, which pay a cent a pound; but we forbear.

We have faithfully compiled the figures in the foregoing Table from the official reports upon agriculture, and commerce and navigation; it is strictly in the form of Mr. Asper's table of cottons, woollens, iron, paper etc., and·if the Revenue Reform theory is true, the existing tariff enables the farming monopolists to steal an immense sum of money from the poor consumers of their products. Of course the theory is false, as the farmers of the country whom it is intended to deceive will readily see when it is applied to their own business.

All well-informed persons know that the tariff on pig-iron no more enhances by the amount of duty the price of the whole domestic product, than does the tariff on potatoes.

Applied to the entire volume of importations and domestic productions, the theory of the revenue reformers produces results which are frightful, atrocious, horrible, and—ridiculous. But it is agony and oratory for the stump, and a big thing in statistics for the tongues and pens of sap heads who are proud of knowing the multiplication table.

JUST after the first snow it struck Bob that it would be well to have a strong two-horse sled, an article he had not provided in the spring when he took the farm near the Corners. Starting to the woods with his axe he met Uncle Noah, mounted, as usual, on the old, blind, bald-faced mare, and looking venerable and wise in his spectacles, to say nothing of the long white hair falling upon his shoulders.

" Good morning, uncle ? "

" Morning, Bob."

" Looks as if we would have winter now, uncle."

" Only squaw winter, there'll be plenty of good weather yet."

" Well, I mean to be ready for snow, I want to make a sled, and am going for the stuff now."

" Ah, Bob, when will you learn wisdom ? You are a farmer, not a wagon maker—why don't you stick to your business ? "

" O, I guess I can make a sled. If the saw-mill was nearer, and I could get the stuff sawed out with less trouble, it would be an advantage; but I have all the tools I want, and John can help me. Of course I can't iron it, but the blacksmith at the Corners is equal to that."

" How long will it take you to get up the wood-work? How much time will you put in it altogether ? "

" You want me to take into account getting out the stuff, taking it to the saw-mill, and back and to and from the shop ? "

" Yes, every thing."

" Well, it'll be about two days and a half, hauling, one way or another, and about two days for working it."

" And two days and a half for the team ? "

" Of course."

" And the ironing will cost how much ? "

" Between six and seven dollars—say six dollars and a half."

" And what do you estimate the wood at ? "

" O, never mind the wood ; throw the wood in."

" My dear Bob, how can you talk so ? You must estimate the wood. What will become of statistical science if you throw the wood in ? "

The man who must go to market pays the price of getting there.

"Well, uncle, say a dollar and a half for the wood ; that'll not be much out of the way, I guess."

"What do you count your labor at, Bob? What is it worth a day, and how much do you allow for the team?"

"John costs me, say, a dollar a day, and I might put my own labor at about two dollars a day, as you want an estimate. In point of fact, my own labor is worth, on an average, as much as that. You may average us at a dollar and a half each, and the team is worth an additional dollar and a half a day."

"Now see what a great folly you were about perpetrating ; Bob, let me state the account :

```
Time spent in hauling, etc....2½ days, at $1.50
Team for same time..........2½ days, at  1.50
Making sled................2  days, at  1.50
                            ——— 7 days....$10 50
Ironing, equal to.........4  days, at $1.50
Tree, equal to............1  day,  at  1.50
                            ——— 5 days....  7 50
        In all $18, or twelve days' labor.
```

And you can go down to Pelham, to the wagon-factory, and buy a better sled for fifteen dollars, a direct saving of about two days, labor, or more than sixteen per cent. of the cost. You would lose no time at all, for you can send down and order it, and it would be delivered, free of cost. There's the argument in a nut-shell, Bob. 'Buy where you can buy cheapest.' You and John are pretty good farmers, why should you turn yourselves into poor mechanics? You never can make as good a job as the Pelham factory. You can't compete with them, and you loose money by trying to. It's an experiment that needs artificial support, for you must work two days at your legitimate business of growing grain to sustain your fancy for sled-making, which is rather costly protection for such a limited manufacture. Don't you think so?"

"I don't know what to say, uncle. Your figures look all right, but it seems to me somehow as if they didn't fit the case. There's some elements in it that you can't set down in figures and add up with the column. In the first place, I haven't had any dealings with the Pelham factory, and they don't know me, and they would want their fifteen dollars cash down. Perhaps they might trust me, on your recommendation, but in the end I would have to pay the cash. Now the blacksmith at the Corners won't want any money from me at all. He'll take his pay in coal when I get to working the bank for my own winter supply. It won't. pay to haul the coal to Pelham, and I couldn't sell it if I did, for they get a better article there for a less price than Jones allows me. I don't count the hauling to the Corners any thing, for I can always get a load of manure to bring back, and drop it on one of the hill fields to the left of the road, the furthest from the barn. Then you know, uncle, that the seeding is through with, and we have some wood to cut and rails to make, but that sort of work is not pressing, besides I mean to work at the sled when the weather is too bad to be out, and when John and I would be sitting around doing nothing, except feeding the cattle and attending to such odd chores; you know I have his wages to pay any how. Then there's the wood that makes such a figure in your account. I suppose it is worth a dollar and a half, as materials for a sled; but if I don't make a sled of it I could only use it for firing, and I have plenty for that purpose. I know it's said figures won't lie, and I always feel daunted by a big column, which foots up all right, and proves itself both ways, but somehow or other the facts do lie—outside of the figures sometimes."

" Well, they're your own facts, Bob—so much the worse for them."

" You don't get off that way, uncle, I know exactly what you are after. I have been reading that free-trade paper published by those foreign mercantile and insurance agents in New York city, which you are kind enough to send me, and I am much obliged to you for it. You think I am 'diverting my capital and labor from the most efficient occupation, to another found less efficient by its need of artificial support,' but I am satisfied that I am effecting an economy of time and labor, keeping out of debt, and helping my neighbor, as well as myself. I am ready to apply my principles to the whole country. The people of the United States ought to produce every thing that they possibly can within themselves; and if it does take more labor, and the product does look a little clumsy at first, it will be a great deal cheaper, when you take into account the thousands of little exchanges and back loads like my coal and manure, and the thousand economies of time, like the use, by John and me, of our rainy days. I haven't got any thing against the Pelham factory, but I can make my own sled, and I mean to do it. When I want a wagon I'll buy it of 'em. I see the free-traders make a fuss about protection increasing the cost of the poor man's axe, and I am a poor man; but I mean to put a hundred dollars into the stock of the axe factory that's going up at the Corners. Have you any stock in it, uncle?"

" Well, no, Bob; I've been thinking about it some."

" I should think you might. It'll be a big thing for you; bring your lots right into market. There'll be thirty hands, most of 'em married men, and they'll want houses. I'll sell some farm truck to them—you bet; and besides, my oldest boy, Noah, your namesake, hasn't enough to do, and I mean to put him to work at the factory. That'll steady him, and give him a good trade, and he'll be under your eye, uncle, so you'll see he don't get wild."

" But, Bob, all sorts of iron and steel manufacture are so very uncertain in this country, up one day and down the next; and I saw it stated on good authority that from the beginning down to this time the manufacturers have not realized more than two per cent. on their investments."

" Whose fault is it, uncle? I say it's yours, for without the support of such respectable and influential American citizens as yourself, this Foreign Free-trade League would soon shut up shop and let our tariff laws alone."

" But, Bob, what would you do? "

" Do? Whenever it was demonstrated that we could produce anything in this country, I would put on such a duty as would keep the foreign article out. We can make axes, I know, for here is an American· axe, and it is the best implement of the kind a wood-chopper ever handled."

" But that would leave the people at the mercy of a few manufacturers, Bob."

" And whose fault is it that we have but a few manufacturers? You are to blame again. You and your free-traders have made the business so hazardous that but few would embark in it. However, I could regulate that. What tariff law was it, uncle, that started with pretty fair duties and then made a regular annual or biennial reduction till it got down nearly to a free-trade level?"

" That was the compromise tariff of 1833."

" I remember, made to conciliate Calhoun and his nullifiers, who ought to have been hanged. Well, since you and others are afraid of immediate prohibition, I would take the '33 tariff and turn it the other way. Make an increase of five per cent. annually for ten years, and provide that ten years afterwards the law should expire by its own limitation, and no duties upon imports should be imposed except for revenue. What do you think of that? Don't you think with such an assurance of stability, home-manufactures would grow faster than the foreign fell away, and under the influence of home-compatition the price would fall a great deal faster than the duty would rise? Don't you think so, uncle?"

Every act of association is an act of commerce.

" Well, Bob, that looks reasonable; but I always thought that the duty on imports was just so much added to the price, and that the consumer had to pay it."

" Did you read the little talk on that subject Mr. Greeley had with the Western member of Congress ? "

" No; what was it ? "

" ' Suppose,' said Mr. Greeley, ' that the duty on imported iron was permanently fixed at $1000 a ton, what would then be the cost of iron ? ' What do you say it would be, uncle, $1080 or $1100 a ton ? "

" Well, no, Bob; I suppose it would be about the cost of making it."

" Just what the Western man said, uncle; though he is reported to have squirmed a little before answering. Now I want cheap iron, and my tariff would make it so cheap, that I am willing to have it repeal itself in twenty years' time, and I believe it would be practically a nullity in ten years; the duty then would be no longer an element in determining the price of the domestic manufacture."

" Well, well, Bob, I must ride on; I am keeping you from work. I ought to have known better than to stir up your combativeness so early in the morning."

" Never mind the time, uncle. There's a deal of political economy goes to the making of a sled by a farmer. A farmer has time to do a deal of thinking, and if he reads both sides, as I do, he's more likely to come out right than a gentleman of leisure, like Uncle Noah, who gets on to his accustomed hobby pretty much as he would mount his old blind mare."

" Come, Bob, don't be impertinent; the mare is a good one, and goes just where I want her to, without knowing anything about it."

" Which is the chief merit in a hobby, as I take it, uncle."

" Well, well, good-bye."

" Halloo ! "

" What is it ? "

" Don't forget that factory stock, uncle; it'll be a big thing for your lots at the Corners."

HOW TO PROVE IT.

"WE have first to prove that we are not fools." The speaker was a woman, who sat in the library attached to an educational institution of which she was Principal. She had just dismissed her Greek class, and had shown her visitor through four Departments in which pupils were pursuing the higher branches of a collegiate education. She spoke earnestly—more than earnestly—with an intensity of feeling which was reflected in the deportment of the young men and women in the school, who needed no monitor, but studied as if they pursued a forbidden pleasure which might, at any moment, be snatched away. We have said that the speaker was a woman, and she was altogether womanly; yet, as she herself said, "less a woman than a negro," and her pupils were of the same race. She was and is doing a noble work, and not only proving that colored people are not fools, but also that they have great aptitude for acquiring knowledge, and are as clever as the whites. And what then? The strong, alert, practical, dominant, fair-skinned people, who do so much of the world's work, have small use for the dead languages, and will not give way to one who comes knowing Greek. We do not mean to say that the acquisition of Greek is useless, or that the zeal for book-learning manifested by the lately emancipated millions of American working-people is misdirected, but we would impress it upon them as forcibly as we may that there is something which is more important still.

Looking upon the pupils of the colored school we mentally asked—when they have learned what their accomplished mistress can teach, and have graduated with honor—what will they do? They present to the mind a question of the destiny of the millions of men and women who constitute the labor element of the Southern States, a question to be pondered earnestly, for it involves not only the well being of a race, but also the peace and prosperity of the country of which they are citizens.

The vast progress of civilized countries, in the present century, is the result of the application of science to the industrial arts, under the fostering care of Government, and in this progress the Southern States of the American Union could have no part, while

---

The trader would prevent association that there may be more need of his services.

their peculiar institution of slavery lasted, for that institution could only be safe and apparently profitable while they kept themselves aside from the industrial life of the world. The slave had to be watched and guarded, and was competent for only the simplest toils. The laws imposed heavy penalties upon any one who would teach him to read or write, and the form of labor in which he was generally employed tended to degrade his sense of individuality. There was the determination on the part of his owner that he should not feel himself to be a man, but one of a herd—the member of a gang—to be driven in mass by the will of a superior.

The South was essentially barbarous, and could not be otherwise while maintaining slavery. It would have nothing to do with the arts which educate the workers of the world and lift them to social position and political power. It preferred, by means of rude labor, to raise crude materials to be fashioned for use by the skilled labor of other countries. It saw in this the only employment it could safely pursue, and it became politically a unit in favor of that National policy which tended to prevent this country from availing itself of the advantages flowing from diversified industries. The South was in favor of free-trade, because it dreaded the growth of freedom, and it dreaded the political preponderance which it feared would result from the development of the industrial arts in the Northern States. A cotton mill nearer to its cotton fields than Great Britain was a perpetual menace.

In 1853 Henry C. Carey published a work entitled "The Slave Trade, Domestic and Foreign; Why it Exists, and How it may be Extinguished." In it he showed how slavery grew and how it is maintained in the United States, in the West Indies; how slavery grows in Portugal and Turkey, in India, in Ireland, and Scotland, and in England; how freedom grows in Northern Germany, in Russia, in Denmark, in Spain, and in Belgium.

These headings of Mr. Carey's chapters signify that people may be really enslaved who are legally free; and the book, which when written was valued as theory, is now vindicated as prophecy. In that part of the book which treats of the United States, Mr. Carey showed that while Protection to Native Industry always, to some extent, existed in this country, at some times it had been efficient, at other times not; and that our tendency toward freedom or slavery had always been in the direct ratio of its efficiency or inefficiency. The politicians of the South knew this truth perfectly well, and knowing that slavery must either grow or decay, and being determined that it should grow, they were hostile to

The foreign market buys by the bushel, the home market by the ton.

the policy of Protection While the country rested in the belief that slavery was in the course of ultimate extinction, the South had statesmen who were Unionists and Protectionists. When the policy of extending slavery over the whole country was adopted, the South had only politicians who were free-traders and Secessionists. In the end there was civil war resulting in emancipation by the sword.

The withdrawal of Southern members enabled Congress to enact the tariff laws of 1861, the exigencies of the Government demanded the passage of the act of 1864; and these laws, in conjunction with the war, which embarrassed foreign trade, gave ample protection to the industries of the Northern States. These industries conquered in the strife. That policy of Protection, which was dreaded by the South because it would have wrought peaceful emancipation, turned the scale of victory in war, and has sustained the finances of the Government in such a way that the evils prophesied at the close of the struggle have been averted, and the country is in the enjoyment of substantial prosperity.

The tendency of the existing policy of Protection is toward freedom and prosperity. As soon as political disturbances are quelled, the beneficent influences of this policy will begin to be felt in the Southern States. The future welfare of the laborers of the South depends upon its assured maintenance, and their participation in its benefits would be hastened by a guaranty that it shall not be disturbed, which guaranty they can themselves give by resolutely and steadily voting in favor of Protection to American industry.

Nothing but the threat of its disturbance for the benefit of the English allies of the slave power can prevent the development of skilled industries in the Southern States. If the policy of Protection is maintained, freedom will grow, if free-trade prevails, slavery, not perhaps in name, but slavery in fact, will be the condition of the laborer. While he has no other occupation than tilling the soil he can never hope to own the soil.

In some parts of the Southern States it has already come to this, that the freedman must sell his labor to his old master, for no one else will bid for it, where the market for his labor is confined to agriculture; and we are beginning to be told by those who would have it so, that freedom to the black man is felt to be a burden rather than a benefit.

To return to the colored school. There was a missionary spirit in it, and the pupils were, perhaps, fitting themselves to teach.

If all tilled the soil, where would be the inventive brain and skilful hand?

They may intend to go South and found schools for the literary education of their own people, and this is well; but we should be better pleased if they could found workshops. Pupil, graduate, teacher, is something, but we may be pardoned for thinking that apprentice, carpenter, builder, or blacksmith, machinist, engineer, is much more.

There is no antagonism of interests between farmer and manufacturer, between the North and the South, between colored laborers and white laborers, or between Southern laborers and Southern landowners. The policy which assures good wages and personal freedom to the laborer, will render valuable the wide tracts of ore and coal, of timber and farm lands, so many of which in the South are now lying dead and profitless. All who live and labor in the United States, as well as all who own property therein, are benefited by the policy of Protection; yet it is most important to the workingman, and upon it the very life of the Southern laborers depends. They may so use the political power they possess as to maintain the freedom which others won for them, and make it a blessing to themselves, to their country, and to mankind.

There will be abundant effort to mislead them, but if they would conclusively prove "that they are not fools," they will strive, in so far as they have opportunity, to master the useful arts and to excel in them, and they will stand firmly in defence of that policy of Protection to Home Industry under which freedom grows and is assured.

Our scene opens in a comfortable old-fashioned log farm-house, situated near the banks of a stream that flows eastward from the outlying broken ridges skirting the Allegheny Mountains. It was in the year 1849, a memorable time in the annals of the long combat waged by home industry against foreign foes and domestic traitors. Sitting by a table, in a dimly-lighted apartment, was an elderly man, in an attitude of deep dejection, who, from time to time, looked up to reply to a younger one, who paced, with nervous steps, up and down the room.

"I'll tell you, father, that I regret nothing," said the young man; "the enterprise was a good one, and we have done our part to ensure its success. When we began here, no one could have anticipated the Government would retract the promise it had made to the iron workers, destroying at a blow the protection which assured us a living profit, and a market for our product. We have fought our fight and are beaten, but not dishonored."

"I can't bear it, Dennis," said the father. "I can't, indeed, and how shall I face to-morrow! The executions will not be stayed—is there no hope of further time?"

"None," said the son; "the attorney for the bank says he has instructions to proceed without delay."

"The bank will buy," said the father, "we will lose the wealth I possessed before I discovered this cursed vein of ore, and the years of faithful labor we have expended in developing it. Ten years from now, or twenty at farthest, the forges and furnace will make some one rich; they will be an immense estate."

"They will ruin some one, you mean, father! In a country where the laws at one time hold forth a promise of protection to industry, and at another deliberately subordinate it to foreign trade, where once in ten years the ruin of manufacturers prostrates all other business, and produces a financial crisis, no great enterprises can take permanent root or flourish. I prophesy that more than one fortune will be lost in the big fossil vein before it makes anybody rich."

"I would not mind it for myself," said the father, "it is your prospects I am thinking of. What will you do?"

The freedom of free-trade is liberty to become enslaved.

A tariff is a tax upon us when levied on goods we cannot produce.

THE NIGHT BEFORE THE SHERIFF'S SALE.

"I'll keep up a bold heart to-morrow to encourage the poor devils, who, having nothing but their labor, are the worst losers by our failure. I'll see the land knocked down to the money-lenders, have the last word with old Grimes, the free-trade black-smith, and then go to New York to begin the world anew. I've lost my fortune trying to make iron; perhaps I can make a fortune by trading in it. I'll try it, anyhow."

"And Ethel?" said the father.

Leaning over him, a slender girl, whose light approach had been unheard, laid her hand upon his shoulder, and said:

"Ethel will remain with her guardian till Dennis makes his fortune, if he will have it so."

A charming morning followed the scene we have just described. The sun and air made a mellow haze, which softened the outlines of the far-off ridges. Clustered about the furnace, which no longer sent forth a busy smoke from its tall stack, was a group of men and women, the occupants of a row of houses that stood near the stream, with small gardens around them. There also were a

India grows cotton and England weaves it.

THE SHERIFF SALE.

number of farmers from the country round about, the lawyer who had the executions in charge, and a deputy sheriff, whose business it was to make the sale.

To these came the proprietors, father and son, whose appearance excited a movement of respectful sympathy, soon giving way to smiles under the cheerful greeting of the younger Mr. O'Neill, who well sustained his promise to bear himself bravely.

Mounting upon a bench in the open air, the sheriff proceeded to read over the long description of properties, and then offered them one by one for sale. As the senior proprietor had anticipated, the bank was the sole bidder, and Vulcan furnace and forges passed into its possession at a sum representing hardly a tithe of their cost.

Glad to be rid of a painful duty, the sheriff, after a few parting words with the O'Neills, entered his carriage with the lawyer, and they were soon out of sight.

Great changes can never at once be realized. A tragedy more fateful in its consequences to many in that little group, than those which move to tears on the mimic stage, had been enacted, yet all had passed so swiftly that its purport had not been understood. The most palpable consequence seemed to be, that the O'Neills had been stripped of lands and home, and were as poor as the poorest men in the group around them, and sympathy with their misfortune was so general that for a moment no word was spoken. Dennis was the first to break silence.

"Well, old enemy," said he, clapping upon the back-a man past middle age, whose leathern apron and smoke-stained visage proclaimed his trade, "your prophecy has come true, and you're likely to get cheap iron without the aid of Vulcan furnace and forges. What do you think of George M. Dallas and the tariff of 1846 now?"

"The same as ever, Dennis; free-trade is right, and if the country wont buy Vulcan iron at a price that will pay for making it, it is because there is a cheaper article in the market. Why should I be taxed to sustain your business, I'd like to know? A tariff on iron is a tax on iron, and the men that buy iron pay it."

"Well, well," said Dennis, "I'm going away to-day, and I'd like to agree with you. I'm sure you're disinterested, for the policy you advocate will ruin you. It is true that you buy iron, but you sell it too, and when I lost my market, you lost yours. The fires are out in that stack, and few of us will see them lighted again."

"What," cried the attentive listeners, "wont the bank start the furnace again?"

"No, the bank will not start it. The bank bought this property cheap, but it will lose money on it. That stack will crumble and fall, the houses down there will be deserted and rot away, and the whole place will be a ruin."

"Wont Johnson still keep his store here?" asked Grimes.

"Johnson will take his stock to the county-seat on court week, and auction it off to the highest bidder. His arrangements are made already. Ask him, if you don't believe me. A month from now, if you want a darning-needle, you must take a day and go to town for it."

"And Stoner's tavern-stand, what will become of that?" asked a ruddy-visaged auditor.

"It will be abandoned as soon as the licence expires," replied Dennis, "for there will be no business to do. There will be no teams hauling coal to the furnace and taking iron away, no hands to board, and no country people to dine and drink at the bar. Stoner will give it up by the first of April, if he stands it that long."

"Why, you mean to scare us," said Grimes; "are the hands all going away?"

"There's Kenney, the foreman; ask him," replied Dennis. "He means to start for the far West, to try farming, and others will be fools enough to follow him. Fever and ague will do the business for some of them, and the others will struggle for a bare living, unless they are lucky, for farming is a trade that is not picked up at once. They'll know how the owners of Vulcan feel to-day, when they get into the hands of the money-lender, and are sold out of their improvements on a mortgage for money borrowed at thirty per cent. It's just about as bad too for those that stay. Hans and Hicks, and Rhodes, and Thomas, and a dozen more of you farmers, have been making money out of the furnace, and improving your land, but you will sell no more timber, and do no more hauling at odd times, nor make wages at coaling when farm work is dull. Potatoes will be plenty and cheap, for you can't sell them to each other, and Grimes can't eat them all, and your butter will be melted and your eggs addled before you can carry them over the mountain to town. Everybody will have to go but Grimes."

"And what," cried a teamster, "will Grimes do?"

"Why, he can't sell his house and shop, and he can't give them away, so he will stay and preach free-trade to the pole-cats that will prowl round this deserted village."

"Good, good," exclaimed a number of voices, "good for him; hit him again."

"Yes, it is good for him, why not? He will get cheap iron, if he carries it on his back from town, but there will be no horses to shoe, and no wagons to iron, and no repairs to make. Food will be cheap, too; potatoes ten cents a bushel, eggs five cents a dozen, butter ten cents a pound, and everything else in proportion, but there will be the trifling drawback, that he can't trade as much as will keep him alive with the half-dozen farmers who will stick about the mountain a year from now. It will be free-trade well illustrated; that is, paying cash till your money is all gone, for what should be had in exchange for your labor, and then burst up, go to smash, starve, or clear out for the Rocky Mountains."

"It's the gospel truth," said one of the farmers, and a nod and exclamation of assent ran through the crowd.

"But," said Grimes, stoutly, "if it's bad for you and me, and this neighborhood, it's better for the country anyhow. You can't deny that."

ALONE WITH THE POLE-CATS.

" I do deny it," said Dennis. " Before we started in to make iron here, free-trade had run up the price of British bars to ninety-five dollars a ton, and some of you will remember how hard times were, and there was very little product of American iron. Well, Congress gave the country a protective tariff, imposing a duty of twenty-five dollars a ton on imported iron, and we started into the business, and I'll say it myself that we have been industrious and careful, and that we ought to have succeeded, and did for a time succeed."

" All can bear witness to that," said Kenney.

" And I will say too," said O'Neill, " that the men we employed were faithful, and honestly earned their wages, and I am sorry they are thrown out of work."

" They'll find something else to do," said Grimes.

" I'm not done yet," replied O'Neill. " The effect of the tariff was to start up the American works, and iron got cheaper in price, but we should have done well had there not been a change in the tariff which cut down the duty to an ad valorem of 30 per cent.,

If a country were made of adamant, free-trade would grind it to dust.

equal as the English iron is valued to about $8 or $10 per ton, and the British manufacturers have lowered the price of bars to forty dollars a ton, for the purpose of breaking us all up. The consequences are that the American manufacturers are ruined, Vulcan furnaces and forges have changed hands, you are all out of employment, and in a year's time property here wont be worth a red cent."

"But the country will get cheap iron anyhow," said Grimes.

"Not so," said O'Neill. "Mark my words. By the time the American iron workers are all ruined, and domestic production ceases, the Englishmen will begin to put up their prices, and the iron that they now ship at forty dollars will cost the people of the United States $70 a ton. It's a bad way to get cheap iron to depend upon but one market to buy it in, and that a foreign market. If you must buy your iron in England, it follows that you must sell to England your grain, or whatever product you have to offer, and then you come in competition with the grain-growing countries of the world, many of which have cheaper transportation to England than you have. Don't you see that under such a system you would find yourselves buying very dear and selling very cheap, and getting less iron for your grain all the time?"

"It's all true," exclaimed a farmer in the crowd.

"However,". said O'Neill, "I didn't intend making a speech, and Grimes shall have a chance now."

"You reason it out very fine," said Grimes, "but it is almost too fine. Every man wants an advantage right away, and he don't care about a profit that goes all over the settlement and waits two or three years before it knocks at his own door."

"You mean to say," replied O'Neill, "that you could get your slice of bread easier if there was no loaf; that a penny near at hand looks bigger than a dollar a little piece away; that it's bad policy to cast your bread upon the water, and that a resolute free-trader is not enough of a Christian to forego an immediate profit for a greater future reward. Well, I'll leave you at that, and here's my hand, for I'll not see you again soon, perhaps never."

"Good-bye," exclaimed one and all, and a voice exclaimed, "three cheers for Dennis O'Neill," which were given with a will, followed by cheers for Kenney, the foreman, and finally with groans for George M. Dallas and the execrable tariff of 1846.

We need not say the prophecy of O'Neill was fulfilled to the letter. The furnaces and forges crumbled away and were wholly obliterated, the village was deserted, and at this day a fallen

Montesquieu says, "Trade is hampered by laws in all free countries."

Brougham said, "England should destroy foreign manufactures in their cradle."

chimney marks the place where it stood. The treasures of the big fossil veins were, until lately, unexplored; even the road through the glen became impassable, while many ships and men were employed in bringing iron into the United ·States, at prices which soon reached seventy-five dollars a ton. It was not until the Morrill tariff and the southern rebellion gave protection to industry that the region again revived, and it is now being demonstrated that the elder O'Neill was a wise and farsighted man, who deserved well of his adopted country, and should have accumulated a fortune instead of ending his days in penury.

A SHORT SERMON.

TEXT.

"The Free-trade League holds that every country has its peculiar natural advantages, and to produce what can be most easily produced in it, and to exchange such products for what is more easily produced elsewhere, is the most profitable exertion of industry."

COMMENT.

THE peculiar natural advantages of a country are limited to natural or nearly natural products. Rice cannot be produced in New Foundland, nor codfish in the waters of South Carolina. The production of these articles would be profitable if there was no trade whatever, their exchange increases the profits of the producer by enlarging his market, and this kind of trade is a useful industry. Whenever nature has not denied the crude material, and manual labor and skill enter into the product of a certain thing, the principal advantage one country possesses over another consists in the superior character and powers of its workers, developed by and developing the special industry. If anything really important is not easily produced, in a country possessing the material, it is evidence of want of education, which can be had only by persistent effort, with the certain result of growth in the producer and product. What is most easily produced is always least valuable, for ice is worthless at the poles, and oranges sell for little near the equator. It cannot be truly asserted as a universal rule that men or nations are most profitably employed in the production which is easiest, for it is often vitally important for them to undertake that which is hardest, if there be reasonable prospect of eventual mastery. Through such efforts the producer rises and the product falls in value.

This proposition, true of the product of the craftsman, is more generally recognized in the domain of art. The peculiar advantages of France, Germany, and especially Italy, enabling these countries easily to produce works of painting and sculpture, must be conceded, but the free-traders have not yet announced that our native artists should close their studios and engage in the production of cotton or corn to be exchanged with foreign countries for painting and statuary. They encourage a slow, costly, and pain-

---

' **The country able to wage war with England prospers.**

ful development of ideal excellence, and neglect the practical and useful arts.

We do not propose to grow oranges in Greenland, or make ice in Florida, though in New Orleans the latter process is found to be profitable, solely because of doing away with the costly machinery of exchange. We would not employ a blacksmith in the construction of chronometers, or engage a sign painter upon works of high art, yet we are glad that these and other artizans are not content to do the things that are easiest for them, but are always trying to do something more difficult, and finding even temporary failure to afford lessons of value, while success is often of advantage to their country and the world.

Suppose we say to the free-traders, we know very well what your proposition means, but why do you not plainly state ·it? Why do you not plainly say that England, France, and Germany possess peculiar natural advantages for the production of iron, cloth, and all textile manufactures, and therefore the United States should relax or abandon the effort to produce these things, and depend upon the more favored countries for a supply? Stated in this way it would at once challenge the inquiry—what is the peculiar natural advantage the United States do not possess? Is it in climate or soil? Our country has every variety of these. Is it the ease with which crude materials may be obtained? The United States have a superabundance of the constituents of almost every manufacture, and indeed the other countries draw from us a great part of their supply. Have we not money enough? Our country is the great producer of the precious metals, and, to make money plenty, we have but to keep our immense annual product of gold and silver at home, instead of sending it all to foreign lands. Has not God given to American workmen the same inventive brains and as dexterous hands as foreigners possess? The sewing-machine, the reaping and mowing machine, and a thousand other American inventions answer this question. Are foreign workmen more familiar with the processes of manufactures, and therefore more efficient? In some cases they are, but this is not a natural advantage, but a matter of education, and American workmen can acquire this knowledge, thus raising the standard of popular intelligence, and also assuring the independence of this country.

But the free-trader at last says, and this is his only point, foreign countries possess a peculiar advantage in having a vast mass of extremely poor workers, who live upon very little and are content with low wages, therefore production is easier there, and the United States should close their workshops and buy the cheap products of foreign labor. Shall we do this? The question must be answered. We must abandon manufactures, or we must reduce the wages of our workingmen to the foreign standard, or we must maintain a protective tariff.

If the wages of labor in this country could be degraded to the level of foreign countries, then, according to the proposition of the free-traders, production would be as easy here as it is abroad. Easy to whom? It would take as much of the toil of the working-man, and he would receive for his share much less of the product. Would it be easier to him? Certainly not. But it would be easier for the non-producer, the official, the money-lender, the trader and speculator, to obtain such products of labor as they need.

Is the production of iron easy in Belgium, where the miners live in miserable huts, and is it hard in the United States, where miners live in comfortable houses?

In point of fact the Free-trade League is not so much concerned for the easiness of production, as for the cheapness of the product, which would appear to be the same thing; but it is not, the difference depending upon the stand-point, as whether you are producing to use or buying to sell again. If it takes no more days labor to produce a ton of iron or a piece of cloth in the United States than in Great Britain, then the production is as easy to the producer, but the product may not be so cheap to others. Perhaps it is relatively as cheap to other producers, as to the cloth maker, or the farmer, but it is more costly to the gentleman of leisure, and to the trader who produces nothing.

Men generally do not get their education in schools or colleges, but are educated by their daily labor. It is therefore an advantage to society and the State that there should be diversity of employments, and especially that such difficult avocations as require skill and ingenuity should be introduced and encouraged as the most efficient means of educating the people. They are better by far than schools endowed or supported by the Government. Better for the reason that the training is such as to advance not only the pupil, but the arts also, and thus industry becomes in time strong enough to sustain itself, and inventions are made which are a boon to all mankind. Whoever will reflect a moment must recognize the truth, that it is not the mission of men or nations to produce that which they can produce most easily, but rather to develop fully all their powers, a condition which is essential to a true commerce.

Free-trade was the father of slave labor.

AS TO A MAN.

Many thousand infants are always painfully learning to write though they will not excel in penmanship, and are much more expert at other things, and they also, at great expense pursue other branches of education without the least hope of equalling the professors and teachers in the arts and sciences. Yet this training is of value, and without a trial, without the protection of compulsory taxes and truant laws, and the bounty of schools and colleges, it could not be obtained, and possibly some pupil will surpass the wisest and most expert teacher, and erect a new standard of excellence. Is it proper for Government to maintain a school, and absurd for Government to maintain a factory?

AS TO NATIONS.

What higher duty rests upon a country than to develop that in which it may be deficient, so that in it the whole frame of learning and the arts may be preserved from decadence, and its independence assured?

The Free-trade League, in announcing its proposition above quoted, declares in effect that the peculiar natural advantage of the United States is the production of food for exportation to other countries, which have peculiar natural advantages for conducting manufactures. The assumption is wholly false, but if it were true, it is well met by the first and greatest of American statesmen, Alexander Hamilton, who says, " Not only the wealth, but the independence and security of a country, appear to be materially connected with the prosperity of manufactures. Every nation, with a view to these great objects, ought to endeavor to possess within itself all the essentials of national supply. These comprise the means of subsistence, habitation, clothing, and defence."

TALK AT THE GROCERY.

"You're all smarter than I am," said Bob to the crowd at the grocery. "I know that you're better posted on financial affairs than the Secretary of the Treasury, and could pay off the public debt right away if you had control of affairs. There's Timmons would end our troubles by taking up the bonds with greenbacks. Benson wants the Government to hold possession of the gold mines and work them for its own benefit. Warner wants to borrow a ship load of coin from Germany, while Brown says, begin with the specie we have in the treasury and pay it out right and left— that's his way."

"Well," said Smith, the grocer, "how would you do, what is your plan?"

"I'd look and see how we got into our trouble," said Bob, "and perhaps I could find our way out. We fell into debt by spending more than our income and giving our bonds for the balance against us on settlement, and we must get out of debt by earning more than we spend, and applying our savings to our outstanding bonds until they are satisfied. We borrowed the money we needed to carry on the war mostly from our own people, and as long as they held the bonds, and the principal and interest were payable to them, the country as a whole was not much worse off; but that's not the case now. The bonds have been traded away to foreigners for iron that we should have made ourselves, and for cloth that we should have made ourselves, and for wines and silks and other luxuries that we might have done without, and the wine is drunk and the other things are about worn out, and now we have got to pay for them, and pay interest until we can pay for them. Foreigners now hold more than a thousand millions of dollars of interest-bearing demands against this country, and the amount is increasing every day. Giving your corn and cattle to the Government to feed its soldiers who are fighting for their country, and taking a 7-30 bond in payment, and then depositing the bond in the treasury and getting National Bank notes for it, and lending the notes to Peters, who starts in and builds his factory, and pays them out to the workmen, and the workmen pay them out to Uncle Noah for building lots, and to you, Mr. Smith, for nails

---

✗ Free-trade condemns labor to mere muscular drudgery.

and lumber, and you pay them to Benson for his timber, and Benson pays the mortgage on his farm, and Uncle Noah puts his notes into bonds again—that's what I call commerce. It brings men together, and starts life and motion in society. In ten years it would re-produce all the cattle and corn represented by the original bond, and as much more in addition, with plenty to eat in the meantime. It makes a national debt look like a national blessing. But if you give your cattle and corn to the Government, and take a bond in payment and trade it off to a foreigner for silks and wines, and then wear out the silk and drink the wine, that is a bad business. The nation may, to be sure, have got value for the bonds by independence assured or victories won, but you have fooled away what you got for them; and not only are you so much poorer, but you have injured your country by forcing it to send to the foreigner for principal and interest of the bond that money, which you and your neighbors are taxed for, and which ought to stay here circulating among our people. That's what I call trade, and that's the way to make a national debt a national curse. Are you any relation to the merchants of your name down at the Cross-roads where I used to live, Mr. Smith?"

" Distant—forty-second cousin, or something like that."

" Well, I can tell you something that I observed down there. Take the case of a farmer that I could name, for it's a true story He was pretty well off, owned his farm at least, and was out of debt, before the Smiths opened their big store at the Cross-roads, within a mile of him. The goods were very cheap, and the merchants were very clever fellows. They tempted him to buy more than had been his habit, and his wife and daughters found it necessary to dress more and better than they had done—discarding homespun for calico, and at last arraying themselves in silks and merinos. The Smiths took all the farm produce at market prices, and took the butter in the fall and did well with it; but clever fellows as they were they always insisted on a half yearly settlement, and it happened that the balance of trade was always a little against the farmer. The Smiths took his judgment-note for the amount, they were clever fellows and in no hurry, but they entered it of record; and so the matter went on until these clever Smiths owned the farm, and the farmer went to the West to begin life anew. You know your cousins are rich, and that is just the way they made their money ; that is the history of more than one farmer near the Cross-roads ; and now after twenty years' trade the Smiths own much of the best land in that settlement.

They had old Sam Bowen in a tight place once, but it happened that when his farm was under execution he got the Sheriff's jury to extend it, and had seven years to pay the debts. The next time Sam was at the Cross-roads the youngest Smith was more ready to sell him goods than ever, but Sam showed no disposition to buy.

" ' Thank'ee,' said he, 'much obliged to you, but I believe I'll not take anything to-day. I've about concluded not to buy any thing I can make on the place until I get those judgments of yours paid off.'

" ' Well,' said Smith, ' here's some prime coffee, you can't make that on the place, let me put up some of it for you.'

" ' I guess not,' said Sam. ' When we wore home spun I could drink coffee, but since we took to buying things we ought to have made, I can't afford to buy the things we ain't able to make. We'll have to use rye coffee awhile.'

" ' I suppose you'll let me have your clip of wool as usual ? ' said Smith.

" ' Maybe some of it,' said Sam. ' Mrs. B. and the girls will have to work enough to keep the family in clothing during the year, and the balance I will hold for the best price I can get. You'll get it, or get the money, Mr. Smith, but not for dry goods; it'll go to pay off the old debt.'

" Smith tried to tempt him with a number of bargains, but it was all of no use, for Sam had laid out his programme and he stuck to it, and the Smiths didn't get that farm. When this country turns in, like old Sam Bowen, to make for itself every-thing it can, and to buy abroad nothing but what it must, we will pay off the national debt, but not sooner, Mr. Smith, not sooner."

" But, Bob," said Mr. Smith, " if we can buy anything abroad cheaper than we can make it here, don't we save money by it ? "

" For several reasons I say not," said Bob. " There's the mis- · chief about buying cheap, that you always buy something you don't want, or get a great deal more than you want. I never go to a vendue without getting into trouble with my wife about some-thing I bring home. It's no use for me to say, ' It's so very cheap, my dear,' for she always answers, ' it's not cheap for us, for we don't need it.' And in point of fact I believe she is generally right. Buying is not the primary thing—production is the first thing to consider. The more we can produce, the less we need to purchase, and the more we are able to purchase. The more we produce, the more we develop our abilities, and grow to power and independence as a people. Even the manufacture of things which are hardest to produce, and dear if made at home, should be greatly encouraged, for it is a spur to invention, a school for the mind and body, and the slightest success is a check upon foreign manufacturers, who otherwise would have the field all to themselves, and who would make cheap things very dear, if no opposition was made or threatened to them."

"Can you give me any facts to sustain that last proposition?" said Mr. Smith.

"Yes, sir, I can; I read the other day in the newspapers, a memorial to Congress, signed by the officers of several important railroad companies, which stated that the mere proposition to manufacture Bessemer steel rails in this country had caused foreign agents to reduce the price from $150 per ton in gold, to $110 per ton in gold. To go back further, Mr. Smith, I suppose you can remember when English lawns sold for about thirty cents a yard, and that their manufacture in this country brought down the price in a year to twelve cents, and finally to ten cents."

"I believe you're right about that," said Mr. Smith.

"It's a great matter, too," resumed Bob, "to consider in what way payment of cheap foreign goods is to be made. All the farmers about this settlement had better pay three times as much for their axes, at the axe factory over the way, as an English axe would cost, for the whole price comes back to them again for truck that they couldn't send to England at all—potatoes, and turnips, and butter, and eggs, and radishes, and blackberries— things that wouldn't be grown at all were it not for the factory, or which would have hardly any price, as was the case before the workmen settled here. I'd like this crowd to tell me how much more butter and eggs are worth now than they were before the factory started."

"Fully twice as much," said Timmons.

"And are axes cheaper or dearer?"

"Decidedly cheaper," said Timmons.

"That's the result always," said Bob, "of bringing together the farmer and the manufacturer. Why, this whole 'buy-cheap and sell-dear' cry of the free-traders is a wretched delusion. If I buy cheap foreign manufactures, what am I buying but cheap wool, and corn, and pork, in the form of cheap labor; my own wool, and corn, and pork, mind you; and I don't buy them cheap without having first sold them cheaper. That's the process of

Labor is the raw material of all industries.

having my corn and wool turned into cloth and iron for me by workmen across the water, three thousand miles away. It's selling cheap and buying dear all the time, and the mischief is that the English cloth and iron-workers don't get the profit out of the transaction no more than I do, that all goes to their rich employers and to the ship-owners, transporters, sailors, brokers, bankers, and foreign agents, and their New York advertising journals, all of whom are such disinterested supporters of free-trade doctrines. It's according to the theory of the whole business that there should be no profit to the English worker, for he must be a cheap man, or the system couldn't be sustained."

"It seems to me," said Mr. Smith, "that you want to do away with foreign commerce altogether, and make another Japan of the United States."

"Not at all, Mr. Smith; I am in favor of commerce in its true sense, which means reciprocity. It's the harmonious blending of diversities—the exchange by independent nations of their own surplus products for such as they cannot grow or manufacture. Its natural track is north and south, across climates—not along them east and west. It carries codfish to South Carolina, and rice to Newfoundland—oranges to Maine, and ice to the tropics."

"But, Bob, if we should make our cloth and iron for ourselves, what would become of the multitude of foreign workmen now employed in supplying us?"

"Mr. Smith, *there are at least fifty millions of people in Europe each of whom would require thirty dollars yearly to make their condition equal to that of our own working classes in this country.* If the policy of European countries were so changed as to give that additional sum to those of their own people who need it, their factories would have a market for their products of fifteen hundred millions of dollars in addition to what they now command, and nearly if not altogether equal to their foreign trade."

"Well, Bob, you argue the question pretty well," said Mr. Smith; "I'll own to that, though I am a bit of a free-trader."

"Give us sufficient protection for twenty years, Mr. Smith, and then maybe I'll be a free-trader, too; but free-trade now means suppression of American manufactures. We know that to be the case from the effects of repeated abandonment of the protective policy by our Government. Now we are all wise fellows together, but I don't think we are quite the equals of the men who founded this nation, and I remember the words of the wisest of them on this subject. Alexander Hamilton says, 'Not only the *wealth*,

Power to labor must be put to instant use.

4

The world at large is benefited by competition for the purchase of labor.

but the *independence* and *security* of a country appear to be materially connected with the prosperity of manufactures. Every nation with a view to these great objects ought to endeavor to possess within itself all the essentials of national supply. These comprise the means of national subsistence, habitation, clothing, and defence.'"

"Well, I guess we had better be moving home," said Timmons; "I know Smith wants to close up."

"No hurry at all, gentlemen; no hurry. Well, if you will go, good-night. Call again."

PROTECTION IN ENGLAND.

THE free-trade doctrines which English agents and agencies preach to the people of the United States are producing their legitimate results where they are put in practice. Belgium is supplying England with manufactured iron; France has supplanted the English silk manufactures; English books are made more cheaply at Leipsic than in London; while English pauperism increases, English commerce declines, and skilled workmen constantly fly from Great Britain to find employment elsewhere. Under free-trade the British workman is brought into competition with the lower-priced labor of the Continent, and must accept smaller wages or emigrate to this country, which has not yet entered into the race for cheapness with the less liberal governments and ruder peoples of the East.

It is not, therefore, singular that there should be a protectionist movement in England, which is not confined to the working classes, but has enlisted prominent politicians, and business and literary men. The *Publishers' Circular*, a leading organ of the book trade, uses the following language in its issue of October 1st:

"The want of reciprocity on the part of other countries is beginning to call up in England the cry of protection, which is heard so loudly in New York and at Washington; and, truly, for our generous efforts we have had but a poor return. English publishers there are who talk of printing their works at Leipsic and importing them into England; and Government itself will, in the next session, have much weight brought upon it for measures to protect all branches of industry. It was only the other day that a huge cargo of ready-made coffins came into the port of London—thousands of coffins, from the smallest size, three feet long, to the largest, fitted in each other, and the interstices filled with wooden spills or pipe-lights—a fit proof that man is but ashes, but a sorry sight for those workingmen who, as undertakers' carpenters, live by our deaths. But so it is; from the cradle to the grave British industry is suffering."

This is a business statement of the matter, and not less significant of the strength of the protectionist party is the cropping out

Man's welfare is the ultimate object of all production.

of their ideas in popular literature. In " Stretton," a late novel by
Henry Kingsley, on page 40 he discusses the question as follows:

"That's just it," said Roland. "Where would free-trade have been
now if it had not been for a combination of perfectly incalculable
accidents? Peel for one accident, the Irish famine for another."

"You go too fast," said Gray. "Who told you that, free-trade
was a good thing except particular cases? I allow that free-trade
in corn is good as it feeds the people; *but free-trade in other mat-
ters is murder to us in this over-populated country.* When we get
a nearly pure democracy we shall have protection to native industry back again, hot and heavy. A pure democracy will never
stand free-trade. When did they ever do so?"

"I don't remember," said Roland.

"I fancy not," said Gray. "Your American and your Canadian laugh it to scorn. There is such a queer *petitio principii*
about it in the first term which seems to me to condemn it. We
practically find that we can compete (having a very rich and
compact country) with every nation on earth on advantageous
terms. Therefore, free-trade is as good for other nations as it is
for us. And so we send our dear Cobden to tell other nations
what he entirely believes—that a franc is as good as a shilling.
Some nations believe him; some don't. The Americans don't,
and they are a trading people too."

We might cite evidence to show that English manufacturers like
Mr. Mundella, M. P., have established factories in Germany and
other countries where labor is cheaper than it is in Great Britain,
and that the evils of unrestrained foreign competition are now in
England being severely felt by employers and workingmen.* Yet
we have in the United States a British free-trade League, officered
in part by Englishmen and wholly sustained by English money, the
mission of which is to import for the consumption of the American
people a Political Economy which, like many of the other wares
England sends us, is entirely too mean for her own use.

---

* In the course of a speech in the House of
Representatives, March 16th, 1872, Hon. Wm. D.
Kelley, of Pennsylvania, said:

"On the 4th of July last my distinguished
friend from Massachusetts [Mr. Hoar] wrote me
from London. His letter was brief, and I can
recall most of it. Among other things he said
that having become somewhat familiarly ac-
quainted with an intelligent workingman, a leader
of his class, he had asked him how the experiment of free-trade was working. 'Fatally for
us,' was the reply, as reported by Mr. Hoar;
'we begin to see how terrible a mistake it was
for the working classes.' Sir, in Pimlico alone I
knew about eight hundred men who made decent
livings by cutting lath; but now all our laths are

imported ready-cut from Norway, and most of
those men are either on the poor-rates or are
earning a precarious living by doing jobs. The
few who were able to have emigrated.' He then
pointed to St. Thomas's Hospital, and mentioned
the facts to which I have referred, and added,
'Sir, but for the fact that the bricklayers' union
would not permit men to lay foreign bricks in London, the very bricks of that building would have
been brought from Belgium, where they had
been contracted for.'"

This action of the bricklayers' union is one of
the most determined and efficient pieces of practical protection which has ever fallen under our
observation, and was quite justified by the circumstances of the case.

GEMS OF FREE-TRADE DOCTRINE.

If the American people had listened to the voice of this free-trade philosopher, in 1842, they would not have the cheap and abundant supply of hardware and cutlery that they enjoy at this time, owing to the duty which has been imposed upon similar goods of English manufacture. Forty years ago American hardware was almost unknown in the trade, yet five-sixths of the consumption is now supplied by home industry. American axes, shovels, spades, and hoes have wholly taken the place of foreign tools, and in cutlery of all kinds, table and pocket, the medium American qualities, which are most suitable for popular consumption, are cheaper and better than those imported from abroad. English journals admit the loss of this trade, and lament it as a calamity. England would prefer to have the American people still tributary to her workshops in Sheffield for knives, saws, chisels, and similar articles of common use. In 1842, Wayland thought it ridiculous to protect the American manufacturers of these goods, but the "high duty" produced results which he could not foresee, and which his disciples declare to be impossible.

Ryland's *Iron Trade Circular*, for March 4, 1871, published at Birmingham, England, says:

" The edged-tool trade is well sustained, and we have less of the effects of American competition. That this competition is severe, however, is a fact that cannot be ignored, and it applies to many other branches than that of edge-tools. Every Canadian season affords unmistakable evidence that some additional article in English hardware is being supplanted by the produce of Northern States, and it is notorious how largely American wares are rivalling those of the mother country in other of our colonial possessions, as well as upon the continent. *The ascendance of the Protectionist party in the States continues to operate most favorably for the manufacturing interest there, and it is no wonder that, under such* BENIGNANT AUSPICES, *the enterprise in this direction is swelling*

To obtain command over nature, man must first develop his latent powers.

to colossal proportions. The whole subject is one demanding the serious attention of our manufacturers."

"As the price of the article is increased, the demand for the article is diminished, there will, therefore, be less of the article produced, because less of it is wanted. By all this diminution is the demand for labor diminished, the price of labor must, therefore, fall, and the stimulus to labor be, by so much, diminished."—*Wayland's P. E.*, page 137.

If, for instance, for any reason, potatoes should continue for several years rising and high in price, Wayland thinks that farmers would not continue to raise potatoes, but would turn their attention to something so much cheaper as to be in little demand, and this same rule would of course apply to blackberries, iron, onions, cloth, etc. When the market for any one of the common necessaries of life is falling and low, Wayland would look for great activity in its purchase and sale, and for a rush of capital and labor into its production; and on the contrary, upon a rising and high market, he would look for great dullness, decline of demand, and cessation of the factory or farm labor engaged in its production. No one ever witnessed such results, and no one having a spark of sense ever expects to; but this simply illustrates the way that things always perversely turn out to be wholly different from that which is promised and expected by free-trade philosophers.

"What is called protection changes only the mode of labor, that is, it takes men from one mode of labor to employ them in another. Suppose, then, that it attracts foreign laborers to one branch of industry, it deters those in another branch of industry from immigrating. If, for instance, manufacturers are protected, this will tend to encourage manufacturers to immigrate, but it will in a corresponding proportion discourage agriculturists."— *Wayland's P. E.*, page 134.

This is part of the staple argument of the free-traders, who constantly allege that the introduction of a new industry robs the old. They assume that the whole people were fully and profitably employed in industries which needed no protection when a tariff either invited or drove them into less productive employments. They never seem to consider that laborers may be out of employment, or to remember the times when men unsuccessfully hunted for work. There have been such times in this country, and we may witness them again, if the efforts of the free-traders to break down our manufactures are successful. In other countries such a condition is chronic. The London *Times* said of agricultural Ireland: "its population is a drug." For many years, in that naturally productive country, the normal condition was nothing to do, and its people were forced to fly from their homes to a land of diversified industries.

The oountry that makes commercial treaties with England is ruined.

Protection which is so efficient as to develop new manufactures creates all the power which operates them. The factory never robs the farm, but always increases its productiveness. The farmer was, perhaps, growing thin crops of grain upon his land ,containing veins of ore and coal which were to him of no value whatever. A protective tariff encouraged a capitalist who had been employed in the importation and sale of English iron to erect ꚗ furnace, which converted the farmer's worthless ore and coal into mineral wealth, from which he obtained a large revenue.

The new industry employed numbers of men who work under the ground, but the surface was not therefore abandoned. The farmer and his neighbors did not leave their occupation and allow the land to lie waste, on the contrary, new lands were brought under cultivation, and new and improved methods of agriculture introduced. Even barren spots were enriched and made productive.

That protection changes the mode of labor is true, but not in the sense Wayland would have us believe. By bringing together the producer and consumer it does away with the machinery of trade and transportation, and may change these modes of labor into some form of productive industry. Wayland admits that the "protection of manufactures induces manufacturers to immigrate," and this would show that protection does not take men from one mode of labor to employ them in another, but rather that it draws skilled workmen to the country where their mode of labor can be most profitably employed; nor is it presumable that circumstances which would draw a colony of manufacturers to settle anywhere would deter farmers from following them. When operatives and traders, clustering together, make a village, town, or city, agriculturists are always drawn to their vicinity. One would suppose from Wayland's philosophy that lands are worthless near growing communities to which workingmen are drawn, and that farmers would want to get as far from such places as possible. Of course this is not the case, and the truth of the matter is well known to every workingman and farmer, but the youths who are so fortunate or unfortunate as to receive collegiate training will not learn so simple a truth from their text-book on Political Economy.

" Exchangers are as necessary to the cheapness of production as producers themselves. The laborer may sometimes complain that the merchant is rich, and he is poor ; that the merchant stands at his desk, while he labors in the streets; that the merchant rides in his carriage, while he travels on foot. But it may be some consolation to him to remember *that were not the merchant rich the laborer would be still poorer,* for every article would be dearer, and besides there would be no one to pay for

---

ⅹ **Free-trade sells skins to England for sixpence, and buys back tails for a shilling.**

The wealthy classes in England desire free-trade in order to keep down wages.

the labor with which alone he is able to purchase it. Were not the merchant to be at
his desk, the poor man would have no labor to do in the street, *and were not the merchant able to ride in his carriage the laborer would be obliged to go barefoot.*"— *Wayland's P. E.*, page 162.

Here now is wisdom in solid chunks and consolation by the
carriage load. Doubtless merchants are worthy men, but laborers
will hardly believe that their condition would be improved by
having more of this class, or by making them much richer than
they now are. It seems never to have struck this free-trade philosopher that if the laborer could buy his shoes directly from the
shoemaker he would not be much benefited by the shoe merchant,
and, indeed, would hardly be justified in keeping up a carriage for
him.

Protection tends to bring together the laborer and shoemaker,
and divides between them the profit which maintained the luxury
of the shoe merchant. Free-trade puts the shoemaker on one
side of the ocean and the wearer of the shoes on the other, and
then lauds the utility of the merchant who makes a fortune out
of a shoe trade which should never have existed.

We reserve for future display other gems of free-trade philosophy which adorn the work now used as a text-book in nearly all
of the schools and colleges of the United States. The stuff is
even taught in institutions of learning endowed by protectionists
for the special training of youth to mining and manufacturing
industries.

TALK AT THE RAIL ROAD STATION.

" THERE don't no farmers get to Congress—that's what's the matter. The Government is run by the manufacturing monopolists and the iron lords, and the people have to pay for it. The farmer pays them a tax on his hat and his coat and his boots, on his shovel and hoe, and his cradle and gravestone—there ain't anything he buys that isn't burdened with taxes for the benefit of somebody else, on the pretext of paying duty to the Government; and what does Government do for the farmer? Nothing! Now, I go for a fair divide. I want a bounty of fifty per cent. on every bushel of wheat I raise, just to make things even. I am an infant agriculturist, and I want protection."

" Ha! ha! ha!" roared the crowd. " That's the talk! Go for him, Jo!"

The man who had fallen into this dispute with a native orator, at a way station on a Western railroad, did not appear a whit dashed by the zest with which his opponent's arguments were received, and the loungers crowded around to hear his reply, with the interest which Western people always take in a public discussion of any question whatever.

" You would hardly have said as much," said the stranger, " if you had known that I am an iron manufacturer."

" No offence was intended," said Jo, " but truth's truth, and I'll stand to it. I don't blame you for taking care of your own interests, and in your place I would do the same."

Stranger. I'll not agree that we have any rivalry of interests whatever, or that my business has been one-half as well and consistently cared for by the Government as yours. Will you allow me the Yankee privilege of asking a question or two?

Jo. As many as you please.

Stranger. What was the amount of capital with which you started into business? I mean what did you pay for your farm?

This question elicited a movement in the crowd, and with visible reluctance Jo answered: " Well, the fact is, stranger, it didn't cost anything in money—I took my land up under the homestead laws."

The working classes in England demand protection to their industry.

When industry is diversified, labor tends to change from muscular to mental.

TALK AT THE RAIL ROAD STATION.

Stranger.　Then the Government made a gift of the capital to start you in business, while I had to scrape and save and borrow money to buy my furnace property. That's a difference in your favor at the outset.　What right had the Government to give you land for nothing that belonged to the people?　Up to this time, at the rates shown in the last report, I estimate· that it has given away about sixteen millions of acres to needy farmers, which would have sold for twenty millions of dollars, and this created just so much of a deficit in the Treasury that I have been obliged to make good by paying stamp tax and income tax and tax on sales to the general Government.

Jo.　Well, the land wasn't worth much to the Government or anybody else when I got it, and wouldn't be now if the railroad hadn't come along here and opened up the country.

Stranger.　How much stock have you in the road?　You and your neighbors must have been taxed pretty heavily to build it.

Jo.　Well, no; it didn't cost me a red cent.

Competition among the buyers of labor is the safeguard of freedom.

Stranger. Any of the neighbors stockholders?

Jo. I believe not. I don't know of any. In fact, like all other roads through the West, it was built by a Government subsidy.

Stranger. Any factories or furnaces along the route?—any manufactures to be benefited?

Jo. Not any.

Stranger. Well, it strikes me that for infant agriculturists you have been sucking away at the Treasury pretty strongly. Nearly the whole amount of land grants for railroad and other internal improvements are a bonus to agriculture. Two hundred millions of acres of the public domain, worth at least two hundred and fifty millions of dollars, have been given away in this manner, and yet you say that Government does nothing for the farmer. I'll venture to say that this very road, built by the Government, has added fifty per cent. to the price of every bushel of wheat you raise, and you have a bigger bonus than any manufacturing interest ever received from the Government. What do you say to that?

Jo. Well, I don't know, stranger. There's something in it; but the Government gets it all back again in the increased prosperity of the country.

Stranger. Take care what you say. You are getting around to the tariff argument, and will be a protectionist before you know it.

Here a laugh arose from the crowd, and Jo, who had been shifting uneasily from one foot to another, was audibly advised to " Cheer up," " Never say die," etc.

Stranger. In addition to the lands appropriated by the Government, there has been money spent and credit loaned to open up the country for you. Some of your Western roads, in which not a single manufacturer was, as such, directly interested, have received not only the odd numbered sections within ten miles of their line, but also a Government loan of from sixteen to forty-eight thousand dollars per mile of road. This is not the end of the matter either.

Jo. You're drawing it pretty strong already, I think.

Stranger. What do you say to the gift, mainly to the Western States, of a hundred millions of dollars' worth of public lands for school purposes? The farmers get the benefit of that. What do you say to the appropriation of ten millions of acres for agricultural colleges? There's the United States Agricultural Department, which has been a tax of millions of dollars upon the Government, and everything it does, from the distribution of seeds to the publication of reports, is a free gift to the farmers of the country.

Jo. Isn't there a mechanical department too ?

Stranger. Yes, there is, and the inventors pay its expenses. They get nothing for nothing. Government patronage of manufacturing and mechanical industry don't cost the people a cent.

Jo. It's right for the Government to introduce new seeds and to send out information to the farmers. It costs but a trifle after all to the whole people, and it helps to build up the country.

Stranger. Did I say it wasn't ? I say it is right, and I approve of all that has been done to encourage agriculture and open up these Western States ; but it is defensible only on the reasons of public policy that justify a tariff for the 'protection of manufacturing industry. And, speaking of Protection, I am reminded that the farmers have not only received the gratuities I have mentioned, but agriculture is also directly protected by the Government.

Jo. Well, there may be some farmers along the Canada line who are benefited by the duties on agricultural products, but they don't amount to much.

Stranger. They amount to that much at least ; but I was not speaking of them. Have you any idea what the Indian policy of the Government costs, and what the expense has been and is of an occasional Indian war, and the constant maintenance of forts and forces on the frontier ? I'll tell you it is a pretty penny, and every cent of it is for the protection of farmers against savages who whould disturb their industry and destroy their property or their lives.

Jo. They don't get the protection as farmers but as citizens. The Government owes it to them.

Stranger. They get it at any rate, and it is right they should have it ; and there is as great need of defence of Home Industry against other foes of the country who have learned how to make trade as ruinous as war. The tariff which does this is no more for the special advantage of a class than the fort which guards our frontiers, and it is as much the duty of the Government to maintain one as the other.

Jo. Suppose I should deny that manufactures are as important to this country as agriculture, what would you say to that ? We could not get along without the product of the soil, for that supports everything else, and not to care for it would be to commit suicide.

Stranger. I should meet you in that case with a weight of authorities of American statesmen, from the time of Washington downward, who have all maintained the doctrine that manufactures are indispensable to the independence and safety of a country, and that they are so important to the farmer that without them he does not obtain a proper reward for his industry. In point of fact the farmers get nearly the whole benefit of the protection afforded by duties on manufactured articles.

Jo. How do you make that out?

Stranger. Suppose there was a vein of iron ore over here on the creek—it would be the property of the farmers, of course, and I'll ask what it would be worth to them?

Jo. Not much.

Stranger. Nothing at all; but get some one to build a furnace over there and it will be valuable. I am paying several farmers twenty-five cents per ton for the ore they allow me to dig and take away at my own cost. That's one profit to them. Then my furnace has given them a market that has increased their revenue from the land at least fifty per cent., and the value of their land has gone up from ten to thirty dollars an acre. That's another profit. They have churches, which they didn't have before, and they have much better schools, and they are all out of debt and doing well. That's not the end of the benefit of my works to farmers, for after we have consumed all the local supply of food we buy Western flour, beef, pork and other products to a large amount. Twenty per cent., or more, of the wages of my workingmen go into the pockets of the Western farmers a thousand miles from the works. What do you think of that?

Jo. If it is as you say, I think you should bring your works out here, where you can get all the food you want, and save carriage both ways.

Stranger. And pray tell me what hinders it except the stupid agitation in favor of free-trade, which scares capital away from investment in manufactures requiring large outlay, and which cannot at once be operated at a profit. You have got good coal over here on Deer creek. I know it, for I have been looking at it, and it is not far to go for a good supply of ore; and I had thought of trying to make iron right here among you, but you seem to be so much in favor of repealing the duty that I'd better not make the investment. I'd better loan my money to some of you on mortgage at twenty per cent. and sell you out after a while when you fail to pay me. That's the kind of business that nobody calls a monopoly. Ah! here comes the train.

Here a score of voices exclaimed: "Are you in earnest now?" "Is there really coal over on Deer creek?" "Never mind Jo, stranger; he never had much sense anyhow." "Whar do you live when you're at home?" "What mout your name be?" "You'll be back again, wont you?" etc., etc., among which the stranger made his escape to the cars, and waved them, from the platform, an amused farewell.

MR. SMITH—we beg his pardon, Cæsar Augustus Smith, Esq.— edited the *Bungtown Guardian* in a creditable manner, and did a very fair business, considering that Bungtown was but three hours' ride by rail from a considerable city, which we will call Chicago.

We say in a *credit*-able manner, for there was little cash in it, but there was a great deal of exchange, by which the editor's wardrobe and pantry, and wood-pile were sufficiently benefited.

However, about the time that the Free-trade League was using its forty thousand dollar subscription to buy up the rural press, Mr. Smith got a new idea, the great idea of British political economy, which is the cheapest article of the kind in the market (so cheap, indeed, that it costs nothing, and the vendors will even pay you for using it); the extraordinary idea which covers all points of faith and practice, which lubricates the wit like British oil, and shines up the intellect equal to British lustre; viz.:

☛ *"Buy where you can buy cheapest!"*☚

Simple, is it not? It seemed so to Smith. It seems so to you, gentle reader, does it not? It's the sort of axiom that might have been made by one of the seven wise men of Greece. Much more appropriate, in fact, to be written up over the front door of the temple, or inscribed upon a corner-stone, than that stupid "know thyself," of Thales, the Milesian.

Smith determined to put this glorious idea in practice.

About this time, also, he devoted the columns of the *Guardian* to the enlightenment of the Bungtowners, on the subject of free-trade, its beauties, economies, etc.

The result may be best shown by reporting a scene which occurred in the editor's sanctum, after the new programme had been in operation for awhile.

Somehow patronage had been falling away, and the *Guardian* was getting into bad case, when Orton, the furniture man, dropped in, in response to a very pressing request to settle his bill.

The foreign industries sustained by us in peace sustained our foes in war.

"No," he said, "he believed he wouldn't continue his advertisement."

"No, he was very positive. In fact he would be d—d if he renewed his subscription to the paper."

"Look here," said Smith. "I don't like to part this way with you; what's the matter? Aint the *Guardian* up to the mark? Why, sir, the political essays in it, its vindication of the principles of free-trade, and its exposure of the selfish schemes of the Pennsylvania iron masters, are alone worth double the price of the subscription. Yet, here you, and others of the best business men of the place, Patton, the grocer at the corner, and Jones, the tailor, and others, have withdrawn your patronage from me. What does it mean?"

"It means just this," said Orton. "That I'm just as good a free-trader as anybody, but I want the trade a little my way. Where did you get the new chairs and desk, with which you have furnished this office?"

"Why, the fact is, Mr. Orton, that I priced yours, but I happened to be in Chicago, and found that I could get them cheaper there, and, well, 'buy where you can buy cheapest' is the first maxim of free-trade. I hope you don't complain of that?"

"Complain! Well, that's cool—that's infernally cool. I advertise a column with you, at a hundred dollars a year, and you make me pay it up in cash, and send the money to that furniture man in Chicago."

"Well, well, Mr. Orton, I had no idea that you would think hard of it, as you are a sound free-trader."

"See here, Smith, I think that Jones remarked to me, when we were noticing your new suit of clothes, that you got them in Chicago. He's stopped his column advertisement, too, I believe."

"Yes, he has; and I assure you I feel hurt by it."

"And, if I don't mistake, Patton was at the station, and saw half a barrel of sugar, a bag of coffee, a box of soap, and a general assortment of groceries, that you had purchased in Chicago. Has Patton dropped his half a column?"

"Yes, he's dropped it, and if you all quit in that way, I can't sustain the *Guardian,* and the principles of free-trade."

"The devil take your free-trade—it's no trade at all for us," interrupted Orton.

"But, Mr. Orton, don't get into a passion, I beg of you. How am I to sustain the *Guardian?*"

Tariffs framed solely for revenue have always proved unsuccessful.

"Passion, indeed. I never was cooler in my life—never. What is it to me, sir—what do I care about it? You'd better take the *Guardian* to your d——d Chicago!"   [*Exit* ORTON.

Mr. Smith cogitated deeply, and the result was that the famous free-trade maxim—

"*Buy where you can buy cheapest,*"

which a lively sailor usually nailed to a tall mast above the editorial head of the *Guardian*, no longer floated in the breeze, but in its stead there appeared a neat group of implements, consisting of the plow, the loom, and the anvil, surrounded with this legend—

⅄ *Patronize Home Industry.*

5

TALK AT THE MILL.

"WELL, Bob," said Uncle Noah, "did you read that copy of the Boston newspaper I sent you with the speeches and proceedings at the meeting, when they organized a Reform League? Did you read it, Bob? Be honest, now; what do you think of it?"

"I think, uncle, that those Boston fellows are a blamed sight smarter than the managers of the New York Free-trade League. The Boston men were protectionists long enough to learn something; they have wit enough and learning enough, and what's more, they have lots of money. About one-fourth of the banking capital of the country is in New England, and Boston handles it. They'll secede pretty soon, I expect, and we'll have to get the South to help us whip them back into the Union."

"But the sentiments, Bob—the arguments—what have you to say to them?"

"Sharp, uncle, and very well put, but all fallacious, and of no account. Your whole pack of free-traders remind me of the young gentleman getting measured for pataloons when a tight fit was the fashion. 'Make 'em tight,' said he, to the tailor, 'very tight; if I can get into them I don't want them.' They want free-trade; any-thing else is stupid; everybody is a fool or a knave that is not in favor of it, and then they admit, that free-trade is a sheer impossibility."

"But the argument, Bob; the argument."

"I'll tell you what I think about that, uncle, once for all. It looks to be a plain, simple argument that a fool can understand. It looks to be true, and it is entirely false. One of the speakers put it plausibly when he said, (wait, I have the paper in my pocket; here it is;) he said, 'Our protectionist friends announce that the world stands ready to flood us with cheap ships, cheap railroads, cheap wool, cheap clothes, cheap leather, and cheap food—all the production of barbarian or pauper labor. They tell us that we shall be hungry, cold, naked, and miserably bound to our barren soil, because of the abundance of everything which will relieve our need, if we let in this bounteous supply.'"

"True, too, aint it, Bob? Isn't that about the position of the tariff men?"

"Not at all, uncle, not at all. The world is not ready to give us a cheap supply of all the manufactured products we need, nor is it bothering itself about the matter. But England, the great trader of the world, wants to go about as far in that direction as Smith, the grocer at the Corners, did, while Carver was running his grocery a mile away at the Cross-roads."

" How do you mean, Bob?"

" Why, you will remember that Carver sold his farm near the Cross-roads, and started a grocery. He laid in a pretty good stock, and did such a business that it hurt Smith considerably. I dealt with him and did well, and a good many others took to dealing, until Smith got alarmed, and put down his prices ten per cent., and then he sold at cost, and finally below cost; and like miserable fools we all left Carver, bought from Smith, and the cross-roads store bursted up inside of a year. You'd better believe, uncle, that Smith put up the prices on us again—put 'em up a good deal higher than ever, and I guess he got all his money back. That's about the game that England is ready to play against American manufactures. It's the game she plays all the time, and I'll match the Boston orator's speech with a statement I read in one of Henry C. Carey's letters. It's an extract from a report made by a Parliamentary Committee to the British House of Commons. By-the-bye I cut it out and put it in my pocket-book, and here it is for you."

"I haven't got my glasses, Bob; I can't read it."

" Never mind, uncle, I'll read it. It is as follows:—' The laboring classes generally, in the manufacturing districts of Great Britain, and especially in the iron and coal districts, are very little aware of the extent to which they are often indebted for their being employed at all to the immense *losses* which their employers voluntarily incur in bad times, in order *to destroy foreign competition, and to gain and keep possession of foreign markets.* Authentic instances are well known of employers having in such times carried on their works at a loss amounting in the aggregate to three or four hundred thousand pounds in the course of three or four years. If the efforts of those who encourage the combinations to restrict the amount of labor and to produce strikes were to be successful for any length of time, the great accumulations of capital could no longer be made *which enable a few of the most wealthy capitalists to overwhelm all foreign competition in times of great depression,* and thus to clear the way for the *whole trade* to step in when prices revive, and to carry on a great business before *foreign* capital can again accumulate to such an extent as to be

Increased productiveness and better markets afford increased wages.

able to establish a competition in prices with any chance of success. *The large capitals of this country are the great instruments of warfare against the competing capital of foreign countries,* and are *the most essential* instruments now remaining by which our manufacturing supremacy can be maintained; the other elements—cheap labor, abundance of raw materials, means of communication, and skilled labor—being rapidly in process of being equalized.' There's the way the world would give the Boston gentlemen cheap things with a vengeance. It puts the argument for sustaining home industry about as strong as I can state it."

"Prejudice, prejudice, Bob, nothing but prejudice."

"Not a bit of it, uncle. Your free-trade doctrine is a cheat on the part of the Englishmen who teach it and pay others for teaching it, and a delusion on the part of the American citizens who accept it and believe in it. It assumes that we were a people fully and profitably employed in farming, when a tariff introduced less profitable manufacturing industries, which abstracted the productive powers of agriculture. That is false. Agriculture can employ but a portion of those capable of working and willing to work, during a part of the time, and the rest is idleness. The introduction of manufactures was not the absorption of old power, but the creation of a new power, which develops and gives profit to agriculture. New industries rarely originate directly from a tariff, but are generally set up as a necessary defence against the exactions of foreign traders, and they need and deserve to be supported as much as the soldier who protects our frontier, or the garrison that guards our coast. Did you ever read List, uncle?"

"Never did, Bob, never read anything."

"I should think not. Well, he says some good things which I have tried to remember. This is one: 'A nation exchanging its agricultural products for articles of foreign manufacture, is like an individual with one arm who invokes the assistance of a foreign arm for his support. Such assistance may be useful to him, but cannot supply the place of the missing arm, for the reason that its motions are wholly subject to a foreign head. It may happen that the efficiency of a man with but one arm is not one-half less, but a hundred fold less than a man having two.' But my grist is done, and I must be off. Good-day."

"Good-bye, Bob. I'll be over to see you soon, and have this out with you."

WHAT IS A TARIFF?

DURING nullification times, in South Carolina, when the tariff was the subject of unmeasured denunciation by all aspiring politicians, the first railroad in the South, from Charleston to Augusta, was built. A couple of honest planters from the up-country were driving quietly through the piney-woods region, when they came upon the iron-track. While they were stopping to speculate and wonder what was the purpose of so novel a thing, a locomotive came thundering along—struck their buggy, knocking it into pieces, and hurling its occupants violently to the ground. Fortunately the sandy soil saved them from broken bones; and, upon picking themselves up, one of them exclaimed:

" Squire, what in thunder was that ? "

" I don't edzactly know," replied the Squire, thoughtfully; " but I've hearn a good deal about a monster they call the tariff, and if that isn't it, I don't know what it is."

It is needless to add that they both voted conscientiously against protection to the day of their deaths.

While we do not suppose any of our readers to be quite as ignorant of the nature of a tariff as the heroes of the above adventure, it may not be out of place or unnecessary for us to give some explanation of its character and functions, and of the terms used in defining different kinds of tariffs or connected with their operations.

It must be understood at the outset that our general or United States Government is a very complicated and expensive piece of machinery. Not only are there numerous civil officers of all grades to be paid, public buildings to be erected and maintained, courts of law to be kept up, and diplomatic intercourse carried on with other nations, but an army and a navy are also to be supported, even in times of peace, and funds must be provided to pay bounties and pensions to soldiers and sailors who have defended their county in war, and to the widows and orphans of those who have lost their lives in its service.

Of course the Government gives more than an equivalent for all these expenses, since it renders services which can only be performed by the united power and authority of the whole com-

WHAT IS A TARIFF?

munity, for the good of the whole community, and money to maintain it is indispensable and must be had, even if it should be necessary to send a United States tax-gatherer to every individual, as most local taxes are collected. During the late war and in the years immediately succeeding it a number of United States taxes were collected directly from the people, but under the lessened expenses of peace these taxes have been gradually repealed, and protectionists are desirous of abolishing them entirely. To give an idea of the cost of Government, we may state that the expenses of the year 1871 for civil purposes, the War Department, the Navy Department, pensions and Indians, and interest on the public debt, amounted to over two hundred and ninety-two millions of dollars. Taking the population of the United States at thirty-eight and one half millions, the cost of Government for that year was $7.50 on each person, or forty-five dollars on each family of six persons. And if the farmer, after paying his last year's State, county, and poor tax to the county treasurer, his road tax to the supervisor, and his school tax to the school directors, had been called on by a United States officer for $45.00 Government tax, he would only have been paying his quota if the whole sum required by the Government should be raised by direct taxation, as is proposed by free-traders. In fact but a small part of the expenses of the Government in 1871 was raised by direct taxes in the nature of stamps, income, etc., and the large sum of two hundred and six and three quarter millions of dollars was raised by the tariff, being equivalent to a contribution of thirty-two dollars and a half upon the quota of tax due from each family of six persons, made by the importers of foreign goods.

There is a story told of an old woman who objected to paying her taxes, and wished to be informed what the Government did with all the money. " It paid the expenses of the Government," said the tax-gatherer. " Why," said she, " I thought it was all paid out of the treasury." She had never studied the question how to get money into the treasury. One of the most difficult tasks of every Government is, to get money into the treasury, and the experience of all nations, and especially our own experience, shows that the easiest method is to charge foreigners, who send their goods into the country for sale, a certain toll for the privilege of so doing. This is the universal custom of all civilized countries, and the tolls so collected from foreigners are called customs, or duties on imports. The statistics of the year 1871, above cited, demonstrate the importance and efficiency of the customs of the United States, as a means of filling the treasury, and paying the expenses of the Government.

Every free country makes just such laws as it chooses for regulating its foreign trade; it sets upon different sorts of foreign goods such different rates of import duty as seem expedient, and makes such rules as it chooses for the admission of all commodities. The law fixing these rates is a tariff law; certain places are named where foreign goods may be brought into the country, which are usually called ports of entry, at each of them the Government has a building for the collection of the import duty or customs, which is called a custom-house, and several officers to attend to this duty, the principal of whom is called, in the United States, the collector of the port.

With each parcel or consignment of goods, a detailed statement of quantity, kind, or value has to be sent, which is called an invoice, and on the arrival of the goods, the custom-house officials have to find by examination that the goods are correctly described by the invoice, after which they must reckon up how

---

A home-market enriches the land; a foreign market impoverishes it.

much money is due to the Government upon the goods, at the rate
fixed by the tariff laws. That duty has to be paid before the
goods are allowed to enter the country, and if it is not immediately
paid, the goods are removed into store-houses, owned or controlled by
the Government, where they are kept " in bond," that is, are held
subject to the duty. Goods thus in bond may be sold, but the
new owner cannot get them until he has paid the duty. Between
forty and fifty millions of dollars' worth of foreign goods are constantly in bond, in United States warehouses, waiting until the
importers or owners find a favorable opportunity to put them into
the market.

When customs duties are assessed according to the value of the
goods imported (being usually a percentage of the value declared by
the foreign invoice), they are called *ad valorem*. When a fixed
sum is charged upon the quantity or amount of goods, irrespective
of value, as if it be so much upon every pound, or yard, or bushel,
or gallon, then the duties are specific. *Ad valorem* duties are easily
evaded, and lead to great frauds upon the revenue. For instance,
a dishonest trader will have cloth, which cost him in England, say
two dollars a yard, invoiced to him at fifty cents a yard, and if
the cloth is subject to an *ad valorem* duty of twenty per cent., he
pays a duty of about 12½ cents a yard, when at an honest
valuation he should pay 50 cents a yard. To successfully
carry through this fraud, it may be necessary for some one to
make oath to the validity of the false invoice, which is so readily
donè, that the worthlessness of custom-house oaths has become
proverbial, and it may also be necessary to give a bribe to the
custom-house officer, whose duty it is to inspect the goods, and
who should be able to discover and expose the undervaluation.

Another method much in use is practised as follows : An intelligent and honest American merchant, engaged in importing goods,
will, from his knowledge of the wants of the market, make up an
order for certain kinds and qualities of merchandize, and send it
to the foreign manufacturer, who fills the order and invoices the
goods at their full value, but, at the same time, makes up a number
of similar lots of goods, which he ships, invoiced at a third, or a
fifth of the true rate, to his own agent in New York city. When
the American merchant offers his goods for sale, he suddenly finds
the same styles in the market at a lower rate than he can afford to
ask, and in the end he sustains a loss, while the English manufacturer and his agent, who are really smugglers, make a handsome
profit by cheating the Government. Owing to this practice, but

---

Organized bodies grow from within; brute matter increases by aggregation.

little legitimate importing is now done, and the foreign trade is generally in the hands of agents of foreign dealers and manufacturers, who can invoice their goods in such a way as to make them liable to the least possible duty. These foreign agents constitute a numerous and powerful body in the United States, and they have established in this country a Free-trade League, which has for its object the regulation of our tariff laws in their interest, and especially the repeal of all specific duties, and the substitution of *ad valorem* rates in their stead.

When a tariff is laid on foreign goods, merely for the purpose of getting money into the treasury, it is called a *revenue* tariff; when it is so adjusted as to sustain and encourage native industries, by affording the workmen engaged in them higher wages than are paid in other countries, it is called a *protective* tariff, and these measures are sometimes combined in what is called a tariff for revenue with incidental protection. Of this last-mentioned character is the existing tariff of the United States.

Every civilized country at this day arranges its tariff in such a way that it will afford direct or incidental protection to its own industries.

England, having a monopoly of machinery for manufacturing purposes, and a very dense population, admits food and the raw material of manufactures free, while raising more than a hundred millions of dollars of her revenue from customs' duties upon such articles as spirits, tobacco, snuff, etc., which are heavily taxed under the excise laws of the kingdom, and are thus defended against foreign products. Her distillers, brewers, snuff manufacturers, etc., could not pay enormous taxes to their Government, if competing foreign products were admitted free of duty.

France has a tariff which imposes protective duties upon manufactures which need defence; and her laws go so far as to prohibit the introduction of many metallic and textile fabrics which would injure or destroy the native industries of the French people. Some of the beneficial provisions of the tariff laws having been lost to the French people through a commercial treaty with England, negotiated by the late Emperor; M. Thiers, the head of the present Government, upon his accession to power, gave the notice required to terminate it.

We might draw further illustrations of this subject from the laws of other nations, and from the history of the civilized countries of the world, which show that intelligent and free Governments have always regulated foreign trade in such a way as to aid and

Diversity of industries and combination of action result from protection.

defend the labor and the business of their own people, and that they
do not repeal protective tariffs until they are no longer necessary.
England, for instance, maintained for centuries protective and
even prohibitory tariffs, which were enforced by the death penalty,
and never abated their rigor until she had attained such superi-
ority in the arts as to make foreign competition impossible.

There are in this country people who profess to be free-traders,
and insist that our Government should abolish all tariff laws, and
raise its revenues by direct taxation. The farmers and workingmen who are engaged in supplying wool, iron, cloth, etc., now pay a
great many local taxes, which must be charged by them as part
of the cost of their product and added to its price, and foreigners
who are exempt from this burden would have a great advantage
were it not for the tariff, which obliges them to contribute so much
toward the expenses of the general Government, that but small
direct charges for this purpose need to be made upon our own
people. To this burden of State and local taxes, borne by our
own industry, the free-traders propose to add the whole amount
of the expenses of the general Government, so that our producers
would be obliged to pay everything, and foreigners nothing!
We hardly think this monstrous proposition will be favorably
entertained by the American people.

There are other tariff theorists, calling themselves revenue
reformers, who advocate a tariff which would be more injurious
than absolute free-trade; for they would raise all the revenues
needed by the Government from duties on tea, coffee, etc., articles
which are not produced in this country, and which are largely
consumed by workingmen, while admitting free of duty every
product of foreign manufacture which competes with home labor.

While we favor economy in all branches of the Government, it
is certain that our country, for some time to come, must have a
large revenue, which will be raised by duties upon foreign goods,
and the example of all other countries, and the results of our own
practice in the past, amply justify our method of so distributing
this tariff upon various commodities as to give home products an
equal chance with foreign, in the markets of our own country. As
foreign countries pay their laborers much less wages than our own
workingmen receive, the amount of import duties charged by the
Government should be at least equal to this difference in wages;
for if this is not provided for, labor in this country must become
degraded, or the important industries which vivify the social and
business life of the people must be abandoned.

 Nine-tenths of what people eat, drink, and wear, is of home production.

The whole of the raw material entering into American manufactures is supplied by American farmers, and amounts in value
to fifty-four per cent. of the product, and the farmers are also supplying food to the millions of workingmen employed in manufacturing industries. The farmer is an equal partner in the production of native fabrics, and in the profits derived from them. It
therefore happens that when wages are low, when workingmen
are unsuccessfully seeking employment, and mills and factories
are at a stand, agriculturists are embarrassed and distressed, and
the country at large is threatened with or plunged into bankruptcy.

The tendency of the protective policy is to encourage our own
people to produce within themselves everything required for their
own use. It enables them to trade with each other instead of
trading with foreigners, to build up their own towns and villages,
instead of adding to the wealth of foreign cities. The benefits of
foreign trade are like the furrow of a ship in the ocean—lost as
soon as made; while the home trade is well represented by the track
of the railroad, which it builds and sustains—a permanent and
ever-growing use and benefit to the communities which it binds
together with its iron bars.

Opposition to the protective policy is fomented by foreigners,
who wish to force our people to trade with them, instead of
being free to trade with each other, and are not satisfied with the
fair chance allowed them under our tariff laws. They object to
these laws, because they dislike to contribute anything for the
support of our Government, and because, under their operation,
the market for foreign commodities becomes constantly more
limited. Our own manufacturers, living among us, find out just
what is needed, and make their goods to suit, and as they constantly
compete among themselves for customers, and invent better machinery and processes, they eventually succeed in driving foreign
products entirely out of our market. Indeed, they do more than
this, for whenever they have adequate protection, for a sufficient
length of time, after supplying our wants, they send their improved
goods to other countries for sale, and in this way American hardware and cutlery, American agricultural implements, and many
other like products, are sold throughout the world, much to the
chagrin of our principal foreign rivals—the English manufacturers. Ryland's *Iron-trade Circular*, published at Birmingham,
England, on March 4th, 1871, says: "The edge-tool trade is well
sustained, and we have less of the effects of American competition.
That this competition is severe, however, is a fact that cannot be

The pretended science of free-trade denies the principle of nationality.

ignored, and it applies to many other branches than that of edge-tools. Every Canadian season affords unmistakable evidence that some additional article, in English hardware, is being supplanted by the product of the Northern States, and it is notorious how largely American wares are rivalling those of the mother country in other of our colonial possessions, as well as upon the continent. *The ascendance of the protectionist party in the States continues to operate most favorably for the manufacturing interest there,* and it is no wonder that under such benign auspices the enterprise in this direction is swelling to colossal proportions. The whole subject is one demanding the serious attention of our manufacturers."

THE FARMER'S QUESTION.

" I WANT you, Bob," said Uncle Noah, " to treat this question as a matter of business—give me facts, instead of glittering generalities."

" Very well, uncle, I'll stick to facts, and I have the authorities right here at hand to show that you are mistaken about the value of the foreign trade of the United States."

" Don't argue from what it is, Bob, under the present laws, but consider, as I do, what it should be and would be under a revenue tariff."

" Very good, uncle; we will go back to the year 1860, in which the value of dutiable goods imported amounted to two hundred and eighty millions, being a higher amount than was ever reached before, and the duty averaged only nineteen per cent. That was pretty nearly free-trade. The exports amounted to three hundred and sixteen millions of dollars, and you would say that the country had done a good business."

" It was a big business, at any rate, Bob, and the farmers made money out of it."

" We'll see about that, uncle. Of our exports in that year, not one-eighth were manufactures. Forty-five and a quarter millions were bread stuffs; and raw cotton, tobacco, etc., made up the bulk of the remainder. Our farmers and planters found a foreign market that year for two hundred and fifty-eight millions of raw-products."

" A great business that, was it not, Bob ? "

" Yes, uncle, a great business; but a small business compared to the whole product of agriculture, which amounted to full twenty-five hundred millions of dollars. We must discriminate, too, between the product of the planter and that of the farmer. Our farmers proper had a product that year worth twenty-three hundred millions of dollars, of which the foreign market took but fifty-nine millions, or one dollar in forty dollars' worth."

" Was it as small as that, Bob? "

" Yes, uncle, it was as small as that. The Western farmers sold in a foreign market but one dollar in forty of their product, while the cotton planters sold abroad three dollars' worth out of every four of their products. That explains, uncle, why the South rebelled and why the West was loyal. Our home business was

---

Free-trade denounces its wretched victims as surplus population.

to our foreign, as forty to one; the planter's home business was to his foreign as one is to three. They preferred an alliance with the Queen of England, or any other foreign power, to union with the Northern and Western States."

" I don't see exactly what you are driving at, Bob."

" It's just this, uncle: Should our farmers seek for a foreign market, or strive to build up a home market? Before the war the foreign consumption of our agricultural products never exceeded two per cent. of their annual value. One more carpenter, blacksmith, shoemaker, or other artisan, in every township of the United States, would give a larger, surer, and better market to its farmers than all the foreign world ever did, or ever can afford them."

" It seems to me I have heard something like that before, Bob."

" No doubt you have, uncle. General Jackson said, in 1824: ' Take from agriculture in the United States six hundred thousand men, women, and children, and you will at once give a home market for more breadstuffs than all Europe now affords us.' We have been building up this home market by encouraging manufacturing industry, and we must continue to do it, for General Grant said truly in his message that ' the extension of railroads in Europe and the East is bringing into competition with our agricultural products like products of other countries.' "

" What are the average sales of our wheat abroad, Bob? What do the foreigners pay for it ? "

" We have no European market for our breadstuffs, uncle, except in Great Britain, and the quantity taken and the prices paid fluctuate in the most remarkable way. In 1860 we furnished the United Kingdom with twenty-nine per cent. of its imports of wheat; in 1865 we supplied but five and three-quarters per cent., and in 1864, for a wonder, we sent thirty-five per cent. of its total receipts. The price of our wheat in England has fluctuated, between 1855 and 1864, from $2.44 to $1.18 per bushel, the average being $1.45 a bushel."

" Is the trade holding up pretty steadily since then, Bob ? "

" It's going down, just as President Grant tells us. In the four years, 1861–4, the British imported from us forty-four and one-third per cent. of their foreign supply of wheat, while in the four years, 1865–8, they took but twelve and three-quarters per cent., getting eighty-seven and one-quarter per cent. of their supply from other countries. The positive decline in quantity was from an average of eighteen and one-half million bushels per annum to a little over seven and one-quarter millions per annum."

"That is startling, Bob. I had no idea the facts were as strong as that."

"President Grant gave the farmers of the country a weighty warning, and they had better see to it that our manufactures are maintained and extended throughout the country. The wages of workingmen must be kept up, so that men will be drawn into mechanical pursuits, and so that skilled laborers from abroad will continue to pour in upon us. It's a poor business to keep the English or German workman on the other side of the water, as the free-traders would do, and feed him there. When the price of wheat is seventy-five cents in central Illinois, it costs the farmer one bushel to send another to Liverpool. The English workman only buys a peck of it in a year, but he buys five bushels of it a year if he comes to the United States; and as for the German workman in Germany, we sell him no American wheat whatever."

"I'm not combating you, Bob. I'm letting you have your own way; but if the foreign market is high or low, big or little, it's a good thing, is it not, as far as it goes?"

"No, it is not, uncle; for it may be, and often is, an unmitigated injury. If $1.40 for wheat at London means seventy cents for the farmer in the West, the reaction of the London price cuts down the price of all that is retained or sold in the home market, though the foreign sales never take off as much as thirty millions of the annual crop, which averages one hundred and seventy-five millions. If the reflected effect of the foreign sales has cut down the price of the whole crop but fifteen cents per bushel, the total exportation is a dead loss; it might as well be cast into the sea, or far better fed to hogs or horses, for one hundred and seventy-five million bushels at seventy cents are worth no more than one hundred and forty-five million bushels at eighty-five cents. That this may, and certainly does happen, follows from the fact that we sell our surplus in a market where we must compete with the grain-growing countries of Europe, in which neither agriculture nor other labor is rewarded as it is in this country."

"Look here, Bob, you seem to be very familiar with this subject. I'd like to know where you get your information."

"You'll find it, uncle, as well as a vast deal of other useful knowledge, in a book entitled 'Questions of the Day, Economic and Social,' by Dr. William Elder. I would advise you by all means to get a copy of it."

A CHAPTER FROM GULLIVER.

SHOWING THE TRUE PRINCIPLES OF POLITICAL ECONOMY, AND HOW
TO MAKE NATIONS PROSPEROUS AND HAPPY.

Apropos to the report for the year 1868, of that finished voyager, Hon. D. A. Wells, Special Commissioner of Revenue, etc., we print a chapter from a manuscript account, hitherto unpublished, of a visit to Laputa, or the Flying Island, made by that equally veracious and adventurous navigator, Lemuel Gulliver, Esq.

A VOYAGE TO LAPUTA, ETC.

CHAPTER VII.

A Further Account of the Academy of Projectors in Logado—A Report on Political Economy—The Author's Admiration thereof.

Passing from the department where the learned man was engaged in extracting sunbeams from cucumbers, etc., we came into another part of the academy, in which the professors are employed by the Government to observe carefully whatever relates to the well-being of the people, as the increase or decrease in fruitfulness of the earth, the operations of trade and commerce, the influence of the arts, the distribution of wealth, and the growth and decay of population; and to recommend such laws as should be enacted for the good of the Commonwealth. The purpose of this institution, as explained to me by the Lord Monodi, my conductor, filled me with admiration. I commended its utility, and asked why its inmates were associated with the projectors, for whom I entertained but slight esteem.

To this his excellency made no answer, but introduced me to the head of the college, who was just completing his annual report, and most obligingly offered it to me for perusal. Owing to its great length I shall not repeat it all, but I was much struck with some of the methods suggested in it for promoting the prosperity of the country. For instance it was clearly demonstrated that the principal wealth of Bilnabarbi consisted in the richness of the earth, and that the inhabitants, instead of engaging in mechanical employments, should rather extract the fertility from the soil by a process warranted to be effectual, and exchange it with the peo-

---

If manufacturing is so profitable why do not the free-traders undertake it?

ple of the island of Luggnagg, for such of the products of the arts as might be needed. The number of ships and men that could be employed in this way was shown to be immense, and the profit correspondingly great.

It was also argued with much force that the encouragement of artificers by the Government was a great injury to the idle and wealthy classes, who were thus obliged to pay high prices for whatever they consumed, and would, therefore, pass over to Luggnagg, where commodities were cheap, to spend their money. The chief professor was, however, greatly the friend of the Bilnibarbi workmen, and to promote their interests he recommended that the tax upon their industry should be increased, and customs duties upon goods brought in from Luggnagg should be abolished. This, he thought, would ensure their prosperity, and he had a number of pages of figures showing that a contrary policy had been most disastrous.

In approaching the academy my conductor had pointed out to me a flourishing manufactory of cloth, and I was much pleased with a street of new and neat cottages, which, I was told, were the property of the workmen. On mentioning this to the professor, he very gravely informed me that it was certainly an illusion, as his statistical table had demonstrated that no such condition of things could possibly exist.

Lord Munodi, who had very considerable estates in the farther part of the kingdom, which he managed according to his own views, then gave the professor a detailed statement of their product, the expense of maintaining them, etc., during a considerable time, and asked him to calculate what would be the result of such management if continued for a period of ten years. The professor readily undertook this task, and presently showed that my host might expect a large increase of his fortune. Upon this his Excellency informed the professor that he was not favorable to the theory of the report, and had managed his estates in a wholly different manner, by greatly encouraging the mechanical arts and diversifying the industry of the people, and that he had been especially careful to see that whatever element of fertility was taken from the soil should be restored to it again. This statement seemed to embarrass the professor not a whit, and he assured us that by altering a figure of his calculation here and there, he could prove to my lord that he might count upon being utterly ruined in about seven years and a half. We, however, begged him not to do so, though he declared that he would regard it as no trouble. This method, he informed us, was very useful, as was, also, a system of averaging everything, which was so elaborate that I confess I was hardly ingenious enough to understand it, or to perceive in what it differed, in the end, from downright guessing, which would have been much easier and quite as accurate.

With respect to the colony of Bulduddrib, which occupies a flourishing city upon the great island of that name, the professor recommended that the inhabitants should be obliged to remove from the city and its vicinity, and disperse themselves in such a way that there should be between every family, the distance of about an English league, as thereby the interests of the merchants who supplied the travelling packmen would be greatly promoted, and there would be little danger of the colonists combining to assert their independence. The wisdom of this policy must be apparent to all, and I shall bring it to the notice of the ministry, that it may be applied to the colonies of Great Britain in the New World.

The professor introduced me to one of his colleagues, a brother to the projector who proposed to abolish the use of language because of its uncertainty and to conduct conversation by means of gestures and exhibitions of sensible objects which every one could carry about with him. This learned man had extended the same principle, and proposed to abolish all commercial bills, notes, and written promises to pay, as well as the use of gold and silver coin, and to make all exchanges in what he called a direct and natural manner. He demonstrated to us with convincing force the injury which plentifulness of money caused to society, and how it oppressed the laboring classes, yet I confess that at the conclusion of his discourse I clapped my hand upon my pocket in sudden fear, and was reassured to find that my well-filled purse was still within it.

Bidding a respectful adieu to these learned men, I passed with my conductor into a large hall, where we rested ourselves for awhile, and here I could not forbear praising the institution we had just visited, and asking what its influence was in the affairs of state.

His Excellency informed me that its principal use was to support the views and administration of the first lord of the treasury, that the salary of the professors was very small, and as they were much courted and feasted by the agents of the kingdom of Luggnagg, it was natural that they should favor the trade of that kingdom. He assured me that for this and other well-known reasons, the recommendations of the annual report had no weight whatever.

THE NEW HERO.

" Every country has its peculiar natural advantages, and to produce what can be most easily produced in it, and to exchange such products for what is more easily produced elsewhere, is the most profitable exertion of industry."—*Free-trade League.*

ONCE upon a time, not a great while ago, and in a country not many thousand miles away, a new hero appeared, and of him a new tale must be written. It will not be like the tales of the old heroes, who were always engaged in some perilous and profitless enterprise, such as digging down mountains, uprooting forests, breasting torrents, releasing captives, resisting enchantments, encountering fiery dragons, or destroying wicked giants. Instead of aspiring, like them, to do the hardest things, and attempting even the impossible, this new hero resolved to do only the easiest things, and thus accomplished more than anybody else. He was a prince, of course, of great strength and noble stature, and he inherited a vast domain, full of fertile farms and streams and forests, and containing mines of gold and silver and precious stones, which had been won from the hostile spirits of the earth, water, air, and fire by his conquering ancestors.

On the day that he came into the possession of his kingdom, he called his council before him, and made inquiry of the condition of his estates, that he might elect for himself and assign to others the easiest labors, and waste no exertions upon doubtful or difficult undertakings. However, the young king soon wearied of the huge volumes of accounts, the endless succession of maps, and the long columns of figures, and said :

" I plainly perceive that my good ancestors—heaven rest their souls—were troubled greatly to maintain their authority, and not only were always doing too much, but were doing the hardest things, and thus wasted their power. Let us begin with the account of what it is customary to do, that I may reject all profitless or useless burdens."

" First," said the chancellor, " upon coming to the throne, the king has always caused to be made complete suits of armor, swords, and great store of other weapons, to be used in the wars, and, at much trouble and expense, numerous workshops are maintained for that purpose. It is said indeed that the heroic founder of your royal line wrought in the smithery with his own hands,

---

Under such protection as we now enjoy, the country prospers.

forging his conquering sword, and that he gave great rewards to skilful armorers."

"A tedious business surely," said the young king, "and most unprofitable. If swords and armor must be had, cannot they be procured elsewhere? Is there no neighboring prince who for cattle or corn will give me coats of mail and such weapons as I need?"

"Truly is there, my lord; yet it was never considered well to depend for these things upon one who may chance to be an enemy."

"Say no more!" impatiently cried the king. "Let the armories be converted into stables for my horses. I shall have gold to purchase all I need."

"Pardon, your majesty," said the chancellor. "Your ancestors had many rich mines of precious metals, yet they have prized iron far above gold, and the utmost toil and care have been expended in its production, and to this end unremitting vigilance is employed to keep the hostile spirits of the earth and fire in subjection. This valuable metal must be followed into the bowels of the earth where the mischievous gnomes have power, and it is but worthless dross until refined and purified by fire and shaped by the toil and skill of experienced workmen."

"Always the hardest things," said the prince. "Am I ever to hear of them? I will have my servants labor no more in iron, but rather seek for gold, with which I can buy all the iron that is needed. The gold or diamonds which one man may find in a single day will perhaps buy all the iron that a hundred men can make in the same time, and surely, therefore, gold-seeking is the easiest and most profitable employment. If the gold should fail, have we not cattle and corn in plenty to exchange for the iron that we need?"

"Alas," said the chancellor, "I fear that the easiest things will become the hardest ere long."

"That is my concern," said the king. "What further industries have we within these realms?"

"Indeed, Sire, many and various are the labors of the people; yet will they be but few and simple if nothing but cattle and corn and gold are produced by your subjects. There are mills, where the corn is ground and made fit for food, which are costly to construct, requiring great quantities of iron, and they must be continually renewed. There are other mills where the wool is prepared for use and woven into cloth by many curious machines and

THE NEW HERO IN COUNCIL.

processes, which employ a large number of skilful workmen, who receive great wages."

"Another monstrous blunder of my ancestors," said the king. "I will send my corn to the neighboring kingdom to be ground, and my wool to be woven into cloth, and thus be rid of the support of such costly establishments and high-priced workmen. Let this privileged class be put upon an equality with their fellows; let them raise corn, or cattle, or seek for gold, and we shall have cloth enough. Let all such hard tasks be abolished, and let it be recorded in the book of the laws that only the easiest labors shall be performed by my subjects, and that whoever shall discover an easier thing shall disclose it to his sovereign and receive a reward."

So the miners came forth out of the mines and sought for lands to till, but they could obtain none, and they sold themselves to the great lords who owned the lands and became their servants. And the workers in cloth and iron came out of their shops and mills and sought for lands, but they had not wherewithal to purchase, and none would give to them, and they also sold themselves to the great land-owners, and became their servants. And presently there came a time when the neighboring kings had so many cattle, and so much corn that they cared for no more, nor would they give cloth and iron in exchange for them; so there were neither implements to till the ground, nor clothing to wear, and even the king was unable to satisfy his wants.

Then there came one to the court who announced that he had discovered an easier thing, which was joyful news, for the easy things had become very hard, and indeed almost impossible.

"Behold!" said he to the king, "you have concerned yourself to produce gold which has failed, and cattle and corn which cost much labor, and now the neighboring kingdoms will have none of them—yet, is there one commodity which they will gladly take and give in exchange all that you desire? In those kingdoms are many employments, exceeding toilsome and curious, and all the men are employed in them all the day, and partly in the night, and the women and children labor also. It therefore happens that a man is the most valuable thing that those rulers possess, and above all things they desire increase of men. Now in your majesty's realm are numberless men who are of no worth whatever, and I therefore propose that you do sell them to the neighboring kings, or exchange them for cattle and corn, iron and cloth, and gold, and all the things that your royal person and court may need. It will not be necessary to set apart more than a certain portion of your subjects for this purpose, and I advise that only those who are tillers of the soil shall be liable to be thus bartered away."

The king thought well of this counsel, and thereupon his edict went forth that· among his subjects all who labored in the fields should be deemed and taken to be merchandize, and might be bartered for cattle, and corn, and other commodities, and lest there should be resistance to this decree, he at once caught and sent away large numbers of them, and exchanged them for swords and armor. He also borrowed of the foreign kings some of their soldiers in whose fidelity he trusted.

Then certain of the miserable tillers of the soil assembled in secret, to consider what they should do, and an old man said :

" I remember when there were mines, and mills, and work-shops; then there was liberty, but now all labor in the earth, and all are slaves. Let us kill this idle and wicked king, and restore our ancient prosperity."

But it appeared that they had no weapons with which to go to war, and knew not how to forge them.

They had been trained and used to do only the easiest things, and so were softened in body and enfeebled in mind.

They were too widely scattered over the country to combine for a successful revolt. No one came forward to lead them.

They therefore concluded that since no better fate awaited them at home than to be sold into slavery, they would escape from the kingdom if they. could, and carry their wives and children with them. At the end of their counsel the old man said :

" Whatever you do, and wherever you go, my children, remember that it is one of the hardest things to maintain liberty, and one of the easiest things to fall into slavery."

"INFORMATION FOR INTENDED EMIGRANTS."

UNDER this heading Ryland's English *Iron Trade Circular*, of September 11th, 1869, copies a New York *Evening Post* article which professes to give the quantity of spool-cotton, felt carpet, poplin, etc., which an equal number of days' wages, in England and in the United States, respectively, would produce. Of course, the *Post*, which is the organ of the British Free-trade League, made the contrast very favorable to England, and the English trade journal quotes it, to quiet the uneasy classes and deter emigration, or, at least, to divert it from the United States to the British colonies.

Perhaps general statements, averages, and even official statistics, have not so much weight as a simple and direct report of one particular case. We have before us a letter, dated in March last, and written by a Mr. Rogers, of Race, Pontypool, South Wales, to his brother residing in a manufacturing town in the interior of Pennsylvania. Mr. Rogers is employed as filler at a blast furnace, and says that he is doing well, earning twenty-five shillings a week, and he gives the cost of living as follows : Flour, 8s. 6d. to 10s. per 56lbs. ; butter, 1s. 6d. per lb. ; cheese, 9d. to 10d. per lb. ; beef and mutton, 6d. to 9d. per lb. ; bacon, 10d. to 1s. a pound.

Furnace filling is a superior grade of labor, usually enabling men to work every day in the month, and to make good wages, when, as is the case in this country, they are paid by the day.

During the month of March, 1869, the fillers at blast furnaces, in the manufacturing town of Pennsylvania, to which we have alluded, each made full time, and $53.01 wages. The prices they at that time paid for the articles of food, named by the Welshman in his letter, were as follows : Flour, $8.50 per bbl. ; beef, 17c. per lb. ; butter, 45c. per lb. ; cheese, 28c. per lb. ; bacon, 21c. per lb.

We have taken the wages and the average prices of the Welsh letter-writer, and turned them into United States currency at the gold average for the month of March of $1.32, and make the following contrast with wages and cost of living in Pennsylvania :

Wages in Wales, per month of 31 days.........U. S. Currency, $35 16
Wages in Penn'a.   "   " 53 01

COST OF LIVING.

	Flour, bbl.	Butter.	Cheese.	Beef.	Bacon.
Wales	$10.25	47½c.	25c.	20c.	29c.
Penn'a...............	8.50	45	28	17	21

The power of creating wealth is more valuable than wealth itself.

With isolated men all pursuits are extra-hazardous.

The respective month's wages converted into either of these five articles would contrast as follows:

	Flour.	Butter.	Cheese.	Beef.	Bacon.
Wales	672 lbs.	74 lbs.	141 lbs.	176 lbs.	121 lbs.
Penn'a.	1222 "	118 "	189 "	312 "	252 "

The excess of the month's wages in Pennsylvania over Wales amounted in flour to 550 lbs., in butter to 44 lbs., in cheese to 48 lbs., in beef to 136 lbs., and in bacon to 131 lbs. The Pennsylvania workman, whose expense account we have examined, had but a small family, and did not buy any bacon in the month of March, and but little cheese; his consumption of the articles we are comparing being as follows: beef, 32 lbs.; flour, 112 lbs.; butter, 11 lbs.; cheese, ½ lb. If we suppose the Welshman to have made the same purchases, he would find but $17.56 in his pocket to apply to other expenses, while the Pennsylvania workman had $37.62 left, a difference of more than $20 in favor of the United States.

In lower and in higher grades of labor we are assured that the contrast would be much better for the United States, and the Welsh furnace filler is not cited as an average case.*

We do not care to painfully examine the statements of the New York *Evening Post* concerning the relative cost of felt carpets, spool cotton, poplin, and pig iron, here and abroad. We prefer to make the contrast upon bread and beef, butter, cheese, and bacon, which our Welsh correspondent seems to think are of most consequence to him. They are the only things the prices of which he cares to quote.

The *Post* article is a specimen of the tricks and impostures of the New York free-traders, who will doubtless be gratified to find it quoted by an English trade journal, as evidence that our country is a bad place for working men.

---

* The following letter confirms these statements in regard to the comparative rates of wages paid to American and English workmen, and is well worthy of thoughtful study by workingmen and employers, as well as by those who demand to know why protection is necessary in this country:—

CAMBRIDGE, MASS., *May* 10, 1872.

DEAR SIR:—A fellow-workman having lent me a pamphlet containing a speech delivered by you, March 16, 1872, against free-trade, I take the liberty of addressing you, as I am interested in that subject. Sir, let us look at the blessings of free-trade where it works so well. I cannot do better than take my own case. When in England I always had a great desire to come to this country, not that I expected to get rich, but wanted to be able to save something for my maintenance in my old age. In 1857 we began to save. In 1864, Mr. H. O. Houghton was in England trying to engage some compositors, printers, and book-binders. I am a book-binder, and applied to him to see if he would pay our passage—myself wife, and two children. He came to Derby, and I told him what I could do. He agreed to advance our passage-money. We had been saving nearly seven years, had twenty-four shillings per week, which was the best wages given. I had saved only £12 10s.

What is the difference between my life there and that which I enjoy here? Mr. Houghton lent me money to buy furniture, and with the passage-money I was in debt

for $270. I received $15 per week first, have been advanced several times; now I have $22 per week. I paid the debt, have my life insured, and $615 in the bank. This has been done in less than eight years. You mention Hon. H. O. Houghton speaking of the compositors of England not being able to pay their passage; there were about twenty in the same shop with me, and not one married man better off than myself.

Since I have been here several trade societies have passed laws for the payment of men's passage to this country, as so few can do so. You speak of the children of the brickyards of Leicester. I have seen them. I worked at the hosiery in Leicester; and had to sew three dozen pairs of children's socks per day, when only about seven years of age. Excuse me for correcting you, but I think you are mistaken in saying that mechanics do not often taste meat there. I have been in Nottingham, Leicester, London, and Derby, and from what I saw I think the mass of the people have meat about five times a week. Allow me to wish you success in your efforts to keep the American public from such miseries as the free-trade policy of England has brought upon the English people. Respectfully yours, JAMES WILSON.

P. S.—I worked with a book-binder who had a large family and only eighteen shillings per week, who told me he had only tasted beef about once in three months; but this is an exception.

HON. W. D. KELLEY.

AGRICULTURE AND MANUFACTURES.

In the debate on the tariff bill, Hon. B. F. Butler, of Massachusetts, said: "I want to say that I never wish to see the time, I never expect to see the time, when manufactures shall flourish in the West; for, sir, *where manufactures largely flourish, there agriculture goes down.*" We quote this language from the *Daily Globe*, which could hardly misreport General Butler, for he seems to have carefully watched and revised his published speeches. The General's worst enemies will accord to him the possession of such great talents as should qualify him admirably for legislative duties, yet even his best friends would be forced to admit, that, as a member of Congress, he exhibits, by turns, unaccountable flippancy, extraordinary audacity, and remarkable ignorance. We do not know which of these qualities should be credited with the statement above quoted, and we will be charitable enough to attribute it to ignorance, with the mental reservation that the General probably knows better.

General Butler would, doubtless, concede that manufactures largely flourish in England, yet the slightest inquiry would teach him that the agriculture of that country has kept pace in productiveness with its manufactures, and he would find that in no country in the world does land possess such great value. There is not a single agricultural product suited to the climate and soil of that country which would not prove this fact. The average yield of wheat for a series of years in England, as stated by the *Journal of the Royal Agricultural Society,* is twenty-eight bushels per acre, an increase during the last century of twenty-two per cent., and a better result than is attained elsewhere in the world. Nor is the quantity produced insignificant, for wheat is grown upon one-seventh of the cultivated acreage of the kingdom. General Butler will agree that in the United States manufactures do not so largely flourish as in England—nothing like it—yet the average yield of wheat in the United States, as given by the Agricultural Report of 1868, was but twelve and one-eighth bushels per acre. A great difference this, and it does not sustain General Butler, but signally confutes him.

Looking at the different States of the Union, we are everywhere confronted by facts which are in startling contrast to General

---

The remedy for all the evils of competition is co-operation.

Competition is of the devil, co-operation is of the Lord.

Butler's views as we have quoted them. Doubtless he will admit that manufactures do largely flourish in Massachusetts, and it should appear that in that State agriculture has gone down. But this is not the case. In the year 1868, the average yield of wheat per acre, in Massachusetts, was 15.5 bushels—a result exceeded by but three States in the Union. It was greater than Illinois, which averaged but 11.5; greater than Indiana, which averaged 11.2, and greater than Ohio, which, owing to the growth of manufactures, has been increasing her productiveness, and attained to an average of thirteen bushels per acre. It may be said, however, that the wheat crop of Massachusetts is not extensive; and that is true; for of the principal crops, Massachusetts grew in one hundred acres but one of wheat, while Ohio grew one in five, and in Indiana and Illinois one acre was wheat in every four that were cultivated.

But looking at the matter in another way, we find that the statement, in the report we have cited, of the average cash value per acre of nine important products of agriculture, inclusive of tobacco, for the whole United States, shows that Massachusetts produced $29.96 per acre, and was surpassed by but one State in the Union. What State was that in which agriculture was more profitable during the year 1868 than in Massachusetts? Was it the great agricultural State of Illinois? Mr. Judd would say so, but he would be mistaken. Was it the new and rich State of Kansas, or of Nebraska? Not at all; nor could Mr. Allison put in a successful plea for Iowa. Was it that wonder of natural fertility and climatic benevolence, the State of California? Indeed, no. It was the little State of Rhode Island—more intensely manufacturing than Massachusetts, for Massachusetts has but 306 cotton spindles to the square mile, while little Rhody has 821, and the average value per acre of the products of her farms, during the year 1868, was $32.70. Agriculture is not going down there.

The average of cultivation in General Butler's State is proportionately as large, compared with entire area, as in the State of Ohio, or in the agricultural States of Ohio, Indiana, Illinois, and Iowa, collectively; so that in Massachusetts agriculture is not only a profitable but also an important industry. It is amusing to hear General Butler assuring Mr. Judd and his Illinois colleagues, who wanted *to vote up agriculture by voting down manufactures,* that *that was the way to do it,* while he knew, or should have known, that in the State of Massachusetts, " where manufactures largely flourish," the average value of farm products per acre is a

Profit lies not so much in producing cheaply as in being employed.

little more than twice as great as in the agricultural State of Illinois.

Try the matter in every way possible, and the result is the same. The horses of Massachusetts are of greater average value than those of any other State. The milch cows are exceeded in average value by but one other State. The sheep are $1.20 per head above the average value of the whole country. The hogs are exceeded in valuation by but one State in the Union. Finally, Massachusetts, according to the monthly report of the Department of Agriculture for January, 1870, is paying the highest wages to farm-laborers of any State in the Union, except California, which has an exceptional labor market, ruling it out of comparison. Strange as it may seem to Messrs. Marshall and Allison, Massachusetts was paying her farm-laborers $39.84 per month, while Illinois paid but $28.54, and Iowa, $28.34. Here is an average difference in favor of the Massachusetts farm-laborer who is represented by General Butler, of $11.50 per month above the constituents of Messrs. Marshall and Allison, who follow the same calling, a difference amounting to $136.80 per year. It would appear that agriculture is not yet going down in Massachusetts.

General Butler succeeded, unwittingly, of course, in stating an immense falsehood in the neatest and most concise manner. He is refuted, not by statistics fabricated for the purpose, but by the reports of the Department of Agriculture, which are readily accessible to everybody, and would abundantly repay perusal by General Butler, or by those other intense friends and champions of the farmers, Messrs. Brooks and Cox, who represent the great agricultural city of New York.

It may be generally stated as a fact, that when manufactures largely flourish, there agriculture does not go down, but flourishes still more largely. It is proximity to the cotton-mill that has made the naturally sterile soil of Massachusetts more productive than the bottom-lands of the great West. It is the development of manufacturing industry that is increasing the agricultural products of the State of Ohio, and also increasing their value. The period of decadence of her agriculture is passed, and with the growth of her manufactures its prosperity is assured.

The product of wheat per acre, in Indiana and Illinois, has fallen below the average product of the United States, which is not nearly one-half the average product of England. This is evidence of exhaustion of the soil, yet these States, Illinois especially, grow an immense amount of wheat. Their agriculture is

"**Satan finds some mischief still for idle hands to do.**"

surely going down, and will continue to go down until they can succeed in diversifying it by cultivation of the roots and fruits for which the mill and the factory make a demand, and this they may hope to do by sustaining a policy under which manufactures largely flourish.

They will learn this after awhile, and when they do they will not send men to Congress who stupidly try to vote up agriculture by voting down the principal market for agricultural products To strike down wages in the United States, and embarrass and suspend manufacturing industry, would be a poor way to benefit the farmers of the West, and it is amazing to find such a policy commended to the Western people as a means of preventing them from engaging in manufactures. They want to manufacture for themselves; they intend to do it, and they are doing it. We fancy that Elgin, with its great manufactory of watches is about as nearly *up to time* as Waltham, and the farmers of Kane county would be disposed to *watch* very closely General Butler, or any other Eastern Yankee who would try to persuade them that the big factory in their neighborhood was going to make their crops fail and their land decrease in value.

THE END.

www.ingramcontent.com/pod-product-compliance
Lightning Source LLC
Chambersburg PA
CBHW021410090426

42742CB00009B/1088